Rezone
and Grow Rich

Rezone and Grow Rich

Millionaire Real Estate Developer Reveals
Strategies To Upgrade Your Health,
Wealth, And Happiness

MICHAEL E. BASH

&

ROBERTA EDGAR

Printed in the United States of America
ISBN-13: 978-0-9992830-2-8
ISBN-10: 0-9992830-2-2

CONTENTS

PART ONE

Rezoning has always been with us, in one way or another.
Take, for example, the following — only *slightly* fanciful
— scenario:

*In the year 2020, the Lord came unto Noah, who was now
retired to a land-locked upscale community somewhere in Mid-
western America. He said, "Once again, the earth has become
wicked and overpopulated, and I see the end of all flesh before me.
Build another ark and save two of every living creature and — if
you can find them — a couple of good humans." He handed Noah
the blueprints for the ark, and said, "You have six months to build
the ark before I start pouring rain for forty days and forty nights.
Good news, maybe, for drought-ridden California, but not so hot
for the rest of the planet."*

*Six months later, the Lord looked down upon the earth and
saw Noah weeping into his Olympic-size swimming pool — but
no sign of an ark. "Noah!" He roared. "I'm ready to turn on the
rain. Where is the ark I commanded you to build?"*

*"Forgive me, Lord," said a contrite Noah, "but things got
complicated. First of all, I needed a building permit. Then I got
into an argument with the boat inspector about the requirements
for a sprinkler system. On top of that, my neighbors complained
that I violated the neighborhood bylaws by building the ark in my
backyard, and exceeding height and density limits. That meant we
had to go to the local planning commission for approval. Then the
city council and the electric company demanded I raise funds for
relocating power lines to clear a path for the ark's conveyance to the
sea. I tried to explain the sea would be coming to us, not the other
way around, but they weren't buying that story. Getting the wood
was another problem. There's a ban on cutting down local trees for*

the purpose of saving the greater spotted barn owl. I tried to convince the environmentalists that I needed the wood to save those owls from extinction, but they weren't having that one, either. Neither was the owl, who frankly didn't give a hoot. And then just when I started gathering together all the animals from around the world, the ASPCA took me to court, accusing me of detaining wild creatures against their will. They also argued the accommodations were too restrictive and that it was cruel and inhumane to force so many of them into so confined a space. Plus, of course, they demanded the appropriate types of bathrooms, in accordance with the comprehensive new gender codes. Then just when I thought I was making headway, the Environmental Protection Agency ruled that I couldn't build the ark until they'd conducted an environmental impact study on your proposed flood. I'm still trying to resolve a complaint with the Human Rights Commission on how many minorities I'm supposed to hire to classify my building crew as sufficiently diverse. Then, too, the Department of Immigration is checking the visa status of those who have thus far applied, and the number that qualifies for a work permit is far too small —
more specifically, zero. Worse yet, the trade unions say I can't hire my sons. They insist I use only union workers with ark-building experience. Not too many of those these days — not after the last time around. On top of that, word got around there would be no overtime, healthcare, or retirement benefits. And to make matters worse, the IRS seized all my assets, charging me with trying to leave the country illegally with a number of endangered species. So, forgive me, Lord, but from the look of it, I estimate it would take at least ten more years for me to get the necessary approvals and finish the ark. And, even then, there's no guarantee."

Suddenly the skies cleared, the sun shone through, and a brilliant double rainbow stretched across the horizon. Noah looked up in wonder and asked, "Does this mean you're not going to destroy the world?"

"No longer necessary, my son," said the Lord. "The government beat me to it."

ຈຈຈ

There is an overwhelming consensus in this world that real estate is the most certain path to wealth. Following are a few testimonials to echo that credo.

ຈຈຈ

The major fortunes in America have been made in land.

~ John D. Rockefeller

Ninety percent of all millionaires become so through owning real estate.

~ Andrew Carnegie

Real estate cannot be lost or stolen, nor can it be carried away. Purchased with common sense, paid for in full, and managed with reasonable care, it is about the safest investment in the world.

~ Franklin D. Roosevelt

Buying real estate is not only the best way, the quickest way, the safest way, but the only way to become wealthy.

~ Marshall Field

Landlords grow rich in their sleep.

~ John Stuart Mill

He is not a full man who does not own a piece of land.

~ Hebrew proverb

Real estate provides the highest returns, the greatest values and the least risk.

~ Armstrong Williams, political commentator and entrepreneur

The greatest investment on Earth is earth.

~ Louis Glickman

ॐॐॐ

INTRODUCTION

ૐ ૐ ૐ

Rezone and Grow Rich is a natural follow-up to my first book, *Evolution by God,* in which I share insights and observations on how to advance the world by creating peace and unity between religion and science. Written on a more personal level, *Rezone and Grow Rich* reveals the novel strategies and tactics I have used over the past half-century to advance as a businessperson and evolve as a human being.

Applied to the real estate industry, the term "rezone" refers to a permit for the reclassification of a property or neighborhood to a more accommodating set of rules and restrictions. As an investor, the primary goal for rezoning is to start with a good property and then modify it to exponentially increase its value in the marketplace.

The first time I encountered this phenomenon was in 1963 at age 32, when I parlayed a mere $1,500 into a $1 million profit — my first of many. Bear in mind that 1963 was half a century ago and that, according to the Bureau of Labor Statistics, $1 million in those days was the equivalent of about $8 million in today's deflated currency.

The early sixties was an excellent time to be rezoning properties, as the baby boomer generation was still in its infancy and young families with tight budgets were in need of affordable housing. Furthermore, businesses were being developed and expanded, commercial properties were in high demand, and the economy was exploding to the upside. Many towns and municipalities were still operating under the original rezoning laws of 1924, which were fast becoming archaic. Mass transportation and improved road systems were making it realistic for large populations to work in the city, while living out their family lives in the rapidly sprawling suburbs.

The following illustrates the simplicity with which rezoning works. Imagine you just bought a new Cadillac automobile for $80,000. I come to visit you, and with a wave of my magic wand I instantly transform your Cadillac into a brand new Bentley that you could easily sell for $200,000. I haven't done anything to the car, mind you — I just waved my magic wand. Such is the incredible power of rezoning and its ability to almost instantaneously generate massive profits.

Chapter One of *Rezone and Grow Rich* describes how fifty years ago I made that first million dollars by applying this process and, in so doing, became what is simplistically called "an overnight millionaire." This first experience unexpectedly turned out so well that I realized I was onto something huge — that, when done effectively, rezoning is relatively low in risk and essentially a safe and profitable investment. The strategy stands in stark contrast to the higher stakes process of traditional building, in which you hire a number of contractors, encounter a series of problems, and are sometimes forced to borrow money against the property. And, then, should you encounter bad times and are unable to pay the mortgage, you lose your entire investment. Not unlike a bad day at the blackjack tables in Las Vegas, but with the squandering of a lot more time and effort.

Over the following decades, I became so proficient at the skill of rezoning I would apply it to every aspect of my life — business opportunities as well as personal and social. As a result, I have strengthened my physical and emotional health, enriched my relationships, enjoyed a balanced and fulfilling existence, and along the way achieved an enduring peace of mind. And it all began with one basic ordinance and, as you will learn, a London Fog raincoat. You can do it, too, and it doesn't require a raincoat. Just a little imagination and a lot of persistence.

One of my favorite rezonings was that of my long-term marriage. The process allowed Arlene and me to evolve from an average husband and wife with normal expectations into a devoted and happy couple living a luxurious and abundant lifestyle. Long after my wife passed away prematurely, I rezoned an average Englishwoman with ambitions of becoming a dentist by paying her way through an American dental school and setting her up in what would become a lucrative private practice. Other women in my life have profited even more extraordinarily, but that's another story. Several, in fact.

In a subsequent chapter, I offer an example of how I successfully utilized the rezoning process outside the field of real estate. In 1979, while riding the elevator of a Manhattan office building, I had a chance meeting with media mogul Rupert

Murdoch and his attorney, and within an hour I had managed to negotiate the purchase of his failing magazine publications and written him a check for $100,000. With that relatively small investment, I quickly turned the enterprise, in which Murdoch had already sunk and lost $12 million, into a profitable operation.

Due to its consistency for success, I began to view my rezoning system as a method for elevating almost anything to a higher purpose. Unfortunately, all too often we overlook opportunities with the potential to change our lives. Either they hide behind a lackluster exterior, or we simply lack the foresight or courage to take them on. Of course, not always will a rezoning meet expectations. Sometimes it takes a rezoning of your *original* rezoning to realize its full capability. Other times, it requires giving it up entirely and cutting your losses. Opportunities exist around every corner, and where one thing doesn't work, another will. My advice is to be in the moment at all times so that you see the possibilities for what they are. But also be assured that whether you notice them or not, they are coming your way on a daily basis. You ought to be paying attention.

If you write for a living, you are familiar with the one word similar to rezoning that strongly relates to your profession: "repurpose." For example, if you've written something for a specific market, there are ways to take that material and, by tweaking it for another audience, essentially infuse it with new life. An example goes something like this: You have written an article on heart disease for a national nutrition magazine and, because it provides steps toward improving longevity, you can now reconstitute it for a magazine geared to seniors, like *AARP* or *AMAC*. Or, with little effort, you can add a diet or exercise routine for a chapter in that health book you are developing for a mainstream publisher.

There are so many ways to use this process in the multiple aspects of your life. Think about it, and let your imagination flow. You can rezone your relationships, your health and fitness levels, your business, your finances, your attitude — anything that you would like to advance in a positive direction, but which has so far refused to budge from its comfort zone.

At my office recently, my business partner watched a short video on YouTube. Using picturesque shots of the earth and the oceans, the presentation made a powerful case for the shortage of premium land on this planet. Slowly, slowly, the video drew the audience toward the beauties of India and argued why this is the perfect time and place to purchase such quality land. Without changing the original images, my partner simply edited the video, replacing the picturesque shots of India with equally dazzling shots of Las Vegas. And the now rezoned video works equally well for selling the Nevada desert as it does for the far more exotic landscapes halfway around the world.

So, whether dealing with land or people or anything else, start with quality and the goal of improving upon the excellence that already exists. That is why I offer the classic example of buying a Cadillac and transforming it into a Bentley, rather than starting with a 30-year-old rundown clunker and 250,000 miles to its detriment. Time is your most precious commodity, so why not use it on those things that have the greatest chance of rewarding you for your effort?

Early in my career, I learned that land zoned for single-family residences is worth considerably less than if it were zoned for multiples. It's a simple case of mathematics — the higher the number of units per space, the greater the value of the property. That is why all the prime property in the 22.82 square miles of Manhattan has greater worth than more sparsely developed land of comparable size throughout the world. Several essential factors come into play, but primarily height and density and the location's desirability. Based on its lifestyle and position as a financial and cultural center, Manhattan has been long considered one of the most exciting cities in the world. Whoever it was that developed the city into the skyscraper capital of the twentieth century set a precedent that few cities in the world have yet to exceed — although international centers such as London, Singapore, Shanghai, Paris, and Sydney are starting to pose a challenge. On the other end of the spectrum, I would guess that barren acreage in the Sahara can still be had for a few grains of sand.

What will a million dollars buy in Manhattan these days? According to www.metric-conversions.org, it will get you a tight 433.25 square feet of living space — barely enough for an adequate kitchen and bath. To reside in the still modest comfort of 1,500 square feet would likely take a minimum of $3.5 million. The small but luxurious city/principality of Monaco, with its world-famous gambling casino, Monte Carlo, is currently considered the most expensive real estate in the developed world at 166.84 square feet per $1 million. So, a Monégasque homebuyer would have to invest well over $8 million for the same 1,500 square feet available in Manhattan for less than half the price. There is no underestimating the importance of location. That is why successful rezoning often requires beginning with the best possible postal zone — one with the greatest potential for growth.

To illustrate the power of my rezoning skills, *Rezone and Grow Rich* provides numerous fact-based examples of opportunities that came my way — how I was able to recognize their huge potential and then develop them to their best advantage. And I didn't stop with real estate. Along the way, I rezoned such distinctive entities as a mountain, a castle, milk cows, magazines, an inexperienced rich kid, and my joyful personal life — which was a rezoning of a remarkably different kind.

Just as important as it is to see the potential for success, it is equally essential to understand and be prepared for the ever-looming possibility of failure. Like many investors in real estate, a man I knew with a net worth of $200 million lost everything. At the pinnacle of his career, he had, let's say, a billion dollars' worth of property, of which eight hundred million was mortgaged. As soon as the billion dollars' value decreased to half a billion, the man's debt exceeded his assets and he was now incapable of paying back on his loan. Instantly, his enormous net worth plummeted to zero. So you see how easy it is to lose hundreds of millions of dollars in the blink of an eye with no immediate way to retrieve it.

In the Talmud, there is a saying in Aramaic: "From a high plateau to a deep hole." And, at some point in their careers, that is where many less savvy investors find themselves — in a deep and dismal hole. They don't have to wind up there and they certainly don't have to remain there. But it is essential to know it exists.

Certainly an investor shrewd enough to have amassed such a large fortune has the requisite skills to earn it all back. But before he can do that, he may be forced to declare bankruptcy, which would mean waiting seven years to regain his credit. He would also have to acknowledge his mistakes — most importantly, to himself — so he can avoid repeating them in the future. I made mistakes of my own in 1974, but, unlike the man I describe above, I was able to retain $2 million worth of the property in which I had been invested, allowing me a path to recovery. Any time I failed thereafter, I was able to rebound because of my natural instinct for self-preservation, which I am convinced I inherited from my father. He had always warned me to keep a tight lid on whatever I was doing and, should I get into trouble, to count only on myself to dig my way out.

Whether in business or personal life, you will sometimes have failures. Although it's easier to start over from a higher level than zero, it's not impossible. I have often told friends and associates they could leave me in a strange city with barely enough for food and shelter, and, given my work ethic, within a few months I'd be back in business and making money. It happens to be my greatest talent and, with a little tweaking of your current methodology, it could also be yours.

In a February 1, 2017, interview ("Michael Bloomberg on How to Succeed in Business") with *New York Times* reporter Sam Porter, former New York City Mayor Michael Bloomberg, whose net worth on February 9, 2018, was listed at $50.8 billion — essentially making him the 7th richest person in the United States and the 10th richest in the world — emphasized the importance of productivity over IQ: "I'm not the smartest guy in the room, but nobody's going to outwork me."

Rezone and Grow Rich addresses rezoning strategies for health, happiness, and world harmony. You will read of how others have followed this path and succeeded beyond their expectations. Also, you will learn tactics for avoiding failure and even sometimes embracing it, as I have done — all the while determining how best to avoid it in the future.

After reading *Rezone and Grow Rich*, you will be able to apply its techniques to your own life and to those of your loved ones and colleagues. By then there will be nothing to stop you from living on a level you never dreamed possible.

To restate my credo: Over the course of your day you are flooded with opportunities for change. Learn to recognize them and know it is within your power to rezone them to their highest potential.

Reinvent — repurpose — ***rezone*** — and reap your rewards. Now, let's get you started.

સ્ર સ્ર સ્ર

CHAPTER 1

HOW I ACQUIRED MY FIRST MILLION BY MAKING SOMETHING OUT OF NOTHING 1958

How to make a million dollars: first, get a million dollars.

~ Steve Martin

ॐॐॐ

My hasty transformation of a leaky basement corner into a landscaped oasis made me a millionaire. And that was just the first of my ventures in a lifetime of lucrative rezonings. But I could not have succeeded without the inevitable smattering of failures, which served as motivation for sharpening my skills.

One thing is consistently true about rezoning — that in order to do it effectively, you must always be seeking ways to improve something to its highest level. This principle works equally well in and out of real estate. No matter what you are doing or where you are going or with whom, be aware of the room for improvement. This cardinal rule remains equally valid whether you are developing land, making dinner, falling in love, getting married, getting divorced, raising children, walking the dog, feeding the cat, flying to the moon, developing a cure for cancer, or just hanging out.

ॐॐॐ

Considering my youth spent tinkering, testing, and trans-forming, my natural inclination was to continue along that path well into adulthood. In 1955, after graduating from the New Jersey Institute of Technology with a degree in electri-cal engineering under my arm, I took an appropriate job with Weston Electric in northern New Jersey at the minimal sal-ary of $80 a week. Over the course of the next few years as a Weston employee, I filed for multiple patents on an equal number of devices. The greatest of my successes would be a recorder dedicated to controlling the temperature of up to twenty-four processes simultaneously. With the use of a ther-mocouple (a sensor measuring temperature), the device would plug into the main system. But, so far, I lacked the right plug.

On the ground floor of the Weston Electric building there were two small rooms adjacent to the reception area. Repre-sentatives from various companies would come in to order equipment, which I would set up for them. Others would visit to sell us their own products. As engineer in charge of applica-tion, I would greet them, examine what they had to offer, and give them a yes or no answer.

One day a man arrived from a company called Cannon Plug. He showed me a special kind of plug with fifty separate prongs, all concentrated in one area. That was it: the precise plug I needed for my device. As soon as I saw it, I asked the man for a sample, took it back to my office, and conceived the new instrument to accompany it. But now I needed a type of pen or stylus to indicate the movement of temperature up and down the chart. The question was how to identify which of the devices the pen was currently registering. To resolve that issue I had to develop a round printer, indicating numbers one through fifty with a dot next to each of them for clarification. The entire setup worked as planned, just as I had imagined. Prior to my invention, each such process had required individual instrumentation, which, collectively, was more expensive, more unwieldly, and took up far more space. To be more specific about the cost factor, a single such appliance was priced at $10,000. Since I made it possible to control as many as 24 of them through a single unit, I was saving a buyer as much as $240,000 (less the original $10,000).

For its application in a number of settings, such as the glass industry and at hospital nurses' stations, the innovation was considered important enough to *Business Week* that they published a feature article on me. As the new wunderkind on the block, I also found my face on the cover of several trade magazines. Published articles praised me for my visionary design and friends and family applauded me for my new celebrity status — "and at such a tender age," they emphasized.

Later on, when Minneapolis Honeywell saw how well the device was selling, they wanted me to assign my patent to their company. But, by then, since I was no longer working for Weston, I was in a position to refuse, which I did. That didn't stop them. They wound up copying it and selling it under their own label.

೧೯೧೯೧೯

Water, water, everywhere, nor any drop to drink.

~ Samuel Taylor Coleridge

In 1959 scientist Alexander Zarchin of Tel Aviv developed a desalination process using water from the Red Sea — part of the Indian Ocean — and, by removing its saline content, he converted it into drinking water. My temperature-control device was an integral component of Zarchin's equipment. This process was of particular importance to Saudi Arabia, with its vast desert region, and to tiny Israel, with its 80 percent desert land mass. It was apparent from the beginning that desalination held potential for eliminating the shortage of drinking water in many parts of the globe where the population was rising, but where access to potable water was not. Desalination plants are now installed all along the Persian Gulf. During the war with Iraq, Saddam Hussein threatened to bomb them so the population would be left without water. Fortunately, he was caught before he had a chance to carry out his threat. Other parts of the world are now using this process, as well. Drought-ridden Southern California has a plant in Carlsbad, one in Santa Barbara, another on Catalina Island, and a number of other locations as far north as Monterey. As of May 2016, several more were proposed for the state and even two in Baja California, Mexico, that would serve a number of Southern California communities. Other parched parts of the globe are bound to follow their lead.

ॐ ॐ ॐ

It was November 1965 when the lights went out in the Northeast all the way up to parts of Ontario, Canada; it became one of the major news stories of the year. There was a running joke for years after, that nine months following the blackout, there was a significant rise in birthrate along the northeastern seaboard. At the time, the two adjacent countries were sharing an energy source and their electrical systems were interdependent. The practical theory behind this coupling was that Canada would be using a majority of the energy at times the eastern United States was not, and vice versa. This worked fine until — it no longer did. One day there was a sudden surge of demand from both countries. Canada and New York State peaked simultaneously, causing the temperature to rise so quickly it became uncontrollable. That's when the system on both sides collapsed. At Weston Electric, my connection with this event was, here again, the temperature control device.

The energy breakdown lasted only a day or so before the system was repaired and restored to normalcy. It was then set up so that, when overload was approaching, the connection between the two countries would automatically separate. So far, it's been over fifty years with no recurrence.

In 1986, following the nuclear accident in Chernobyl, I saw video footage on TV showing that my instruments had been used in their Russian laboratories. I also saw them connected with several patients at Jerusalem's Hadassah Hospital.

Before being replaced by digital technology years later, my invention was used in any number of applications across the globe, providing me with a great boost in confidence so early in my career.

Get a Mentor

Considering that the device was responsible for contributing an estimated $40 million to Weston's annual bottom line, you would think they would have offered me a big corner office and a fitting raise in salary. Well, at least the raise in salary. In reality, they gave me a paltry increase of $10,000 a year, no doubt to ease their collective conscience. I thought to myself, *They're making millions on my invention, and I get a lousy bump of $192.71 a week? Not smart of them to underestimate me … but far stupider for me to ignore.*

That was the moment that defined my future and taught me a lesson about creative control. It was now past time for me and my innovative mind to venture into a landscape where we would be better appreciated and able to retain legal ownership of our innovations. I silently thanked my employers for their wake-up call.

But now, what?

I asked my father for his routinely sage advice. He said, "As you know, I import building materials to Israel … but on the side, I am a builder. You can start doing the same. Then, when you begin making more than your current salary, you quit your job and begin working for yourself. That's how it's done."

It sounded logical enough, so that's what I did. I swallowed my pride and continued to work as an engineer at Weston from 8:00 a.m. to 4:00 p.m. Mondays through Fridays. Then, after hours, I morphed into a builder-in-training.

When starting a new career — in fact, when starting a new anything-you-know-nothing-about — you are encouraged to find someone of experience willing to share their expertise with you.

The year 1958 was notable for the birth of my first son, David, but also for my entry into real estate development.

My budding career began when my father's American CPA, a man named Soffer, offered $5,000 to partner with me in my brand new Sabra Development Company, along with another $5,000 from one of his colleagues. So there I was with $10,000 of other people's money to invest in building a house, and yet I could barely distinguish a hammer from a buzz saw. All I knew with certainty was that real estate was my future. And since building a house required owning the land on which to build it, the first thing I had to do was seek out a broker. So, I scanned the Poughkeepsie Yellow Pages for "real estate brokers," but the list was so long it was hard to eliminate all but one. Then I saw the name Charles Patrick, which almost leapt off the page. I thought, *Wow, that's an Irishman.* And I had a weakness for the Irish. During Israel's War for Independence, a number of Irish nationalists joined us in our fight. Why, you might ask? For one thing, the Irish loved a good fight. For another, they particularly loved fighting the English. We were happy to give them the opportunity.

I called Charlie and agreed to see him on Sunday after church services, but I wondered why I was meeting an Irishman at a Greek Orthodox church. Later on, he explained to me that Patrick was not his real name — that it was merely an English version of Papageorgiou. About fifteen years older than I, Charlie had worked as a broker before he began buying and developing land. Considering our immediate rapport, he volunteered to help me launch my new career. The first thing he did as my mentor was sell me a piece of property he owned in LaGrange — a city adjacent to Poughkeepsie, where he resided in a beautiful home with his equally beautiful wife. I accepted his asking price of $45,000, even though I could initially offer him only the $10,000 I had from my new associates. The remaining $35,000 I would pay him at the rate of $5,000 a year over the next seven years. He agreed, and we were now in business.

When, later on, it was time to connect the property with the main road further down the hillside, Charlie introduced me to a man named Alexander, who deferred his $10,000 fee until after I had built and sold off the entire acreage. Slowly but surely, I paid Alexander back his $10,000, and became debt-free. I was fortunate to be associated with such accommodating professionals.

Those were different, simpler times in the financial markets. There were no FICO or credit agencies to monitor financial dealings. Loans were made through introductions — referrals — either from another bank or from someone substantial in the community. Charlie Patrick was my "someone substantial," and in order to get the bankers at Poughkeepsie Savings and Loan to approve my construction loan, he persuaded them they could "trust this guy" — that I knew what I was doing. It was on Charlie's recommendation and the fact that I looked older than I was and talked a good game that they agreed to the loan. What they had done by entrusting me with so much money was akin to granting an 800 FICO score to a toddler in diapers. In effect, I became a living example of how "beginner's luck" and "ignorance is bliss" can work in tandem to generate a new universe out of little more than a vacuum.

Even though I had been born with a knack for things electrical and mechanical, it was Charlie Patrick and the crash course he gave me in real estate development that provided me with the rezoning of my young lifetime. Charlie had come along at the precise time that I needed him, and he taught me everything he knew about land acquisition and development. Eventually he would sell me other properties, always at a good price. He also shared his banking and other connections with me, and he secured construction loans for me based on his personal approval.

Why did Charlie take such an interest in me, when I had no tangible evidence to show for my potential? I would like to think it was because I was young and ambitious and that he could sense a profitable future with me. I also think he was fascinated by my differences, in the way I spoke and thought. He quickly discovered I was a fast learner and constantly proving his instincts right about me — about my being trustworthy and a hard worker.

With no small credit to Charlie, I was soon building my first house for the price of $25,000, a beautifully decorated hillside model home of 2,200 square feet. This would be the first of a tract of single-family homes I would build on Charlie's former property. Appropriately called High Acres, the homes would all benefit from dramatic views of the surrounding mountains, like something out of a dreamscape.

As a newbie to real estate and with not one dime to spare, I was out to prove to myself how perfect a house I could build within my strict budget, and even have a few dollars left over to pay myself a small fee. Since any respectable home at that time demanded wallpaper on every wall, I covered every square inch, including the ceilings. By the time the papering project was behind me, I could enter any room in the house and feel as though I were cozily ensconced in a lavish oversized jewel case. Another prerequisite for new homes at the time was the sunken living room, a feature that provided the allure of stepping elegantly up into the dining room so that a few feet further along you could step elegantly down. The kitchen contained all the usual essentials, including a refrigerator/freezer that was not included in the price of the house. Décor for the square-shaped bathroom was my own innovation. I used an abundance of imported Italian marble in black and green — like something out of a 1970s Woody Allen movie echoing the 1930s. The Roman bath was stylishly sunken, surrounded by a planter with assorted live flowers, and topped with an adjustable waterfall to inject a degree of exotica. An ivory-colored phone installed next to the tub provided a blend of convenience and luxury in those pre-wireless days — along with an overhead tanning lamp to give outsiders the illusion that you, the affluent owner, did your wintering in Palm Beach. To assure the illusion of privacy, the window was made of one-way glass.

Considering my painstaking efforts to create a luxury home for a middle-class family, you will understand why I regarded what happened next to be on par with a national emergency.

かかか

Beginner's Luck

Necessity is the mother of invention.

~ Plato

It was four months after I had broken ground that the model home was complete and ready, or so I thought, for public viewing. I was proud of my maiden accomplishment, and breathed a grateful sigh of relief that the effort had transpired without major calamity. But then, just two days before open house and while taking a final inspection of the basement, I was shocked to find a conspicuous leak in a remote corner of the recreation room. Why hadn't I noticed it before? My immediate instinct was to call in the maid for a cleanup, thinking that would be the end of it. But as she was mopping up the puddle, the stream of water continued to seep in from one of the edges. That was the moment the first wave of panic overtook me. There was no way I could show a model house with a leak in its recreation room — and yet there was no time to make the repair.

I found out later on that, due to the high water table in the area, it was common for basements to leak. So for subsequent homes in that tract, I would build a system around each basement from which a pipe would run all the way down to the roadway, where it would connect to the storm sewer four and a half feet underground. I was learning on the job — as much from my mistakes as from my achievements.

So there I was with the leak in the basement, knowing I had minutes left to save my professional reputation — the one I had yet to acquire. All of a sudden, the imaginary light bulb switched on in my head, and I thought to myself, *What exactly am I? Well, I'm an inventor, of course. So, what am I going to do with the leak? I'm going to reinvent it. And fast.*

Reinvention required my building a short brick wall around the leak and filling the space with dirt, which would allow the water to seep inside from underneath and become quickly absorbed by the soil. Next, thanks to the basement's high ceiling, I was able to plant the affected area with a live tree, which I bordered with colorful flowers. The final effect was so beautiful that it appeared to have been borne of genius — rather than of sheer desperation and a ticking clock.

⥤⥤⥤

Unlike California, where homes were built on slabs, eliminating the option for basements, foundations in the East were typically built four feet underground. That allowed for extra living space, fully functional windows, and the vitamin D sunshine a newly embedded plant needed for its survival. Now, instead of representing a flaw, the rezoned leaky corner added a quirky kind of charm to the house and even helped to convince a man named John Dow and his wife that this was the home of their dreams. Over the years that followed that sale, I had an occasional twinge of guilt, wondering if the owners had ever caught onto my scheme or if the leak ever flooded their basement. Three decades later, while I was showing my brother, Yigal, around the area, we drove by the house, which, by now, was surrounded by the rest of the housing development. I immediately recognized an older John Dow standing in his yard. Unwilling to let this opportunity slip by, I got out of the car and approached him. "John, do you remember me?"

John smiled, "Yeah. You're the builder who sold me this place."

"Have you and your wife been happy here?" I worried about his answer.

He said, "Absolutely. It's a great house."

Unwilling to confess my guilt for no reason, I said, "By the way, that planter downstairs ... it was kind of a new idea of mine at the time. How did you like it?"

"Oh, we love it. We've had lots of vegetation growing in there since then ... all kinds of trees. And the best part is, we don't even have to water it. It's completely self-sufficient."

John Dow and I shook hands, and I drove away with a smile on my face. My beginner's luck hadn't left me.

ॐॐॐ

Once the model home found an owner, I began selling out the rest of the acreage, basing the newer houses on the original, but cutting a few fiscal corners along the way. And because I never built any of the homes until I had sold the property on which they stood, I had no need for additional investment money throughout the development process.

The personnel director at my office was one of my first buyers, so I gave him an excellent price. My reasoning was that, based on the deal he got, he would naturally recommend me to anyone new to the company who might be in search of housing. I could even hear the imaginary conversation flitting through my mind. *"Hey, Joe, the wife and I are in the market for a home, but we haven't a clue where to look. Got any suggestions?"* And Joe would say with a grin, *"Matter of fact, I just bought a great little place from this guy, Michael Bash, for an unbelievable bargain price. Give him a call and tell him l sent you."* Then he would hand his new employee my business card, and I would take it from there.

Unfortunately, soon after he moved in, Joe's house sprang a leak like the one in the model home, and the bulldozer I used to repair it wound up crashing into his basement and breaking down the entire wall. Although I managed to get it fixed in the long run, the short run proved a bit dicey. Fortunately for me, that nasty little incident did not discourage Joe from recommending me to incoming employees, just as I had envisioned. What helped was that I was becoming adept at giving a little to get a lot back.

After every lot was sold and all the homes inhabited, I agreed to purchase the sixty adjacent acres from Charlie Patrick, which, in turn, were adjacent to three hundred and fifty acres, also belonging to Charlie. The land had been an unharvested apple orchard — its potential completely untapped and its overripe apples scattered about in varying stages of decay. Charlie charged me $190,000 for the apple orchard, and my father brought in a partner to put up the money. Keep in mind that I had not only found the property and made the deal, but I was also investing the benefit of my newly acquired expertise, plus my time and energy. Since my investor was only supplying the finances, he was perfectly willing to accept my terms, which was to put up the entire $190,000 — leaving me with a financial risk factor of zero. I told you I was a fast learner.

In the end my investor made a lot of money from the project — and why? He had had enough foresight to recognize an opportunity when he saw it and to seize upon it — even though, from the outset, the financials were skewed against him. His investment of funds and my investment of time and effort worked in our favor. Here's the math: While the original cost of each acre was $500, that same acre was costing Matthew Pines twice that much, at $1,000 per acre. But five years later each of those acres was worth $10,000. Not a bad return on investment for either of us. Like High Acres, these were also high lots with excellent views, but the houses were much bigger at 4,000 square feet each.

෨෨෨

By 1960 I was financially stable enough to quit Weston. But I was immediately rehired by the new owners as a consultant — and, ironically, at the same salary I had been getting for full-time work. I chose to name the new Weston instrument on which I was consulting "God Willing." The new company owner liked the idea. He said, "Now that we're introducing God into the picture, it's bound to succeed."

Mainly due to the influence of my grandfather, a Talmudic scholar, I had a tendency to "bring God into the picture" every chance I got. And it has never failed to work for me throughout my life. How could it? This is God we're talking about.

Rezoning for Love

One rainy Thanksgiving night in Manhattan, after leaving the home of friends with pounds of roast turkey and trimmings under my belt, my car and I had a nasty accident heading from the George Washington Bridge to Newark, New Jersey. A couple of days passed before I woke up in a hospital bed in Jersey City, staring into the bright blue eyes of a beautiful blonde nurse. She would have been shocked to learn that morning that she would soon fall in love with me and eventually become my wife. From our first conversation, Arlene made it clear that she had no expectations in life other than a traditional home and family. Fortunately I had the next couple of weeks of hospitalization in which to convince her that she deserved a lot more — a big house, dazzling diamonds, an exciting lifestyle, and best of all, *me* — even on my paltry paycheck of $80 a week. Level-headed realist that she was, Arlene merely shook her head and smiled. "Don't promise me anything. I'm happy the way I am." But with my stubborn drive for improving anything that crossed my radar screen — especially the woman I now loved — I persisted from my sick bed until I finally won her over. Not long after we married, I managed to deliver on my promise — the house, the diamonds, and the exciting lifestyle. I also inspired Arlene toward education and philanthropy, and a full and enriching existence that included my love and devotion. She never looked back, except with appreciation. Or so she assured me on a regular basis.

And there, in brief summary, you have my recipe for the successful rezoning of the woman you love into the fabulous femme you knew she was all along. If I could succeed in rezoning Arlene from our humble beginnings — especially considering she was engaged to another guy when I met her — you could do it with your own partner of choice. And it does not have to include material things, which are the least essential of the ingredients. What is important is that you nurture her to reach her full potential and provide the requisite love and support. This formula works equally well for men as for women.

Caveat: In the case of rezoning humans, do not attempt the strategy on anyone who is resistant. No matter how high-minded your intentions, everyone retains the right to determine their own fate, however self-defeating or sloppy you might view their efforts. Ultimately, it is not for you to play God. That's His (Her?) job.

Rezoning Dutchess County

Drive eighty miles north of New York City and you find yourself in the City of Poughkeepsie. Capital of Dutchess County. This town of an estimated 32,000 (2010 census) is known as home to the distinguished Vassar College, whose student body in 1963 was still restricted to women. Typical of September, the weather was hot and sticky, particularly oppressive inside city hall that day when I pleaded my case for a rezoning ordinance. The city council was in session discussing my application, which was being loudly opposed by a group of 250 members of the community — mostly women.

My application involved a twenty-acre property that was currently zoned for one home per acre, which I hoped to redevelop for sixteen apartment units per acre — three hundred twenty units in a total of forty buildings. With my few years of experience building single-family residences, I had decided the timing was right to move into building apartment units. In uncertain times when people realize they can no longer afford the upkeep or mortgages on their homes, they tend to scale down and move into apartments. During this period, the trend became so prevalent, it was known in the industry as "the decade of apartments." As my first such project, I had bought this property for $80,000, with a meager $1,500 down, along with the caveat that I be given three to four months to secure the remaining $78,500. The owner was a lawyer and he was willing to facilitate the process by handling all the legalese, which saved me the cost of hiring my own attorney.

The exciting thing about rezoning a property previously zoned for single families is that the instant it is approved for multiple units its value skyrockets 1,000%. Therefore, a property currently worth $100,000 would a millisecond later be valued at $1 million, without adding so much as a blade of grass. In this particular case — and cases vary dramatically — it didn't take much effort on my part to secure the authorization.

The City of Poughkeepsie was divided into wards or sub-areas, and this particular piece of property was located off Innes Avenue, in an old section of town. Most of the concerns expressed by the protesting group were that this was a single-family home community and that my project would crowd the area with too many children, too many buses coming and going, and would ultimately create a serious shortage of classrooms — the usual no-growth arguments. I assured them this development would infuse the neighborhood with fresh air and probably even raise the real estate values. They weren't listening. Convinced as I was about the trend toward multiple-family units, the burden was on me to persuade those naysaying others to see my point of view.

WIIFM

In the week leading up to this meeting, I left little to chance. As a way of assuring myself of majority backing from the homeowners of adjacent properties, I brought their attention to an old, unsightly incinerator and chimney, which had once been used to burn the communal garbage. Not only had it been a non-functioning eyesore for some time, but, I warned them, it would be more noticeable were it surrounded by single family dwellings, each perched on an entire acre of land with little to distract attention from its hideous presence. What would that do to their real estate values? By contrast, my more realistic plans called for greater density in the form of low-priced apartments — renting at $90 for one-bedrooms and $115 for two. In such a massive development an incinerator like this, gross as it was, would hardly draw attention. I assured them that, considering all the property's negativities, my solution made the most sense. To clinch the deal, I made a proposal to all those neighbors in the adjacent twelve properties with their shallow lots. I said, "With your approval, I'll be in a position to give you a bit more land for your backyard so you can accommodate a swimming pool or a volleyball court or a barbecue pit, or anything that appeals to your particular lifestyle — even a granny flat. And I won't charge you a dime."

Now, the amount of land I was willing to donate amounted to maybe one acre in total, which still left me with nineteen acres and in no way compromised my plans. On their side, however, these homeowners were instantly won over by my generosity, and were delighted to send letters of praise and approval to the city. The gist of the letters was positive: "We are the neighbors directly adjacent to Mr. Bash's property, and we approve his plan to build those apartment units."

The strategy worked. I had based my plea for approval on the classic principle, WIIFM (What's in it for me?). And I told them exactly what *was* in it for them — what I was willing to give them in exchange for their cooperation. This was not to be construed as a bribe, just the business of doing business. But I still needed more insurance. So thanks to my friend, the city manager, I was able to meet beforehand with certain council members as well as the mayor.

Expectations of rain on the day of our pre-hearing meeting convinced me to wear a London Fog trench coat. One of the council members kept staring at it until he could no longer restrain himself from asking where I had bought it. "No problem," I told him as I took it off and handed it to him. "Keep it. I know where to buy another." The council member welcomed the coat into his loving embrace and smiled his appreciation in silence. From that moment on, I knew I had his vote. Now, considering that I needed a majority — three out of five — I had two more votes to go. The rest of the meeting went according to plan, with promises made and subsequently delivered.

Throughout my presentation on the day of the public hearing, I stressed the merits of the project to the city and assured the residents they would experience no negative impact. I also explained how it would infuse new life into their moribund neighborhood, potentially increasing its real estate value — the classic argument. But their indignation continued to escalate. Finally my dad, on his annual visit from Israel, turned to me and said, "Michael, you'll never get this resolved in your favor."

Considering my close relationship with the city manager, I felt more confident than I otherwise might have been. So I said, "Dad, relax. It's going to happen."

Dad was not convinced. "Michael, you're only thirty-two. You haven't been through this routine as many times over the years as I have. Listen to them. They're angry. The council would be crazy to vote for you."

After hours of hearing heated objections, the four-member council and mayor were finally winding down the proceedings and getting ready to vote. Wiped out from the heat and nervous anticipation, I had been keeping myself busy by blotting my brow, loosening my tie, and wishing myself back home under a cool, refreshing shower.

Finally, after everyone had had a chance to express his or her outrage, it came time to vote. The mayor voted against me, as did the council member in charge of that ward. The other three voted in my favor. So, as if we had robbed a bank and gotten away with a shitload of cash, my father stood and whispered, "Let's get the hell out of here. These women will eat us alive."

With only three or four months to come up with the $78,500 purchase price of the property, I drove to Manhattan to meet with three wealthy investors, one of whom was Joseph Kushner, a Holocaust survivor with the telltale numbers tattooed on his inner arm. As successful as he would become in building a vast real estate empire, future generations might recall him best as grandfather to a boy named Jared — who would not only follow successfully in his footsteps, but would go on to become son-in-law to the forty-fifth president of the United States, Donald Trump, and dedicated husband to Ivanka, as well as father to their three children.

Around that same time, my father introduced me to an Israeli named Moses Moses, a foreman by trade, who was well acquainted with two builders from Czechoslovakia — the Rausman brothers. Although the brothers traditionally worked in New Jersey, they were willing to partner with me in New York. Out of the $750,000 they gave me as their 50 percent share of the project, I paid the nearly $80,000 due on the property, and pocketed the rest.

In order to get the construction funding, Charlie introduced me to the president of the Poughkeepsie Savings and Loan. I told him my goal was to build the first fifty apartment units out of a planned total of three-hundred and twenty. He told me this was a single-family home community and I would never rent those apartments. So, no — no loan. The first thing I did in the aftermath was call the Rausmans in

Manhattan with the disappointing news. They sent me to meet with an executive at New York Life, who agreed to consider lending me the money based on approval by a company inspector. I worried about what the inspector would think of the defunct incinerator and the wall I had built to hide it behind. But luck was with me the day he showed up. Poughkeepsie had just experienced a blinding blizzard and the entire land surface was blanketed with a thick layer of snow. Nothing was visible to the naked eye, objectionable or otherwise. The executive at New York Life was satisfied with what little he saw and said he would lend me the money on one condition, that "instead of just building the first fifty units, you build all three- hundred twenty." This was a jarring proposal. I was building my first group of multiple dwellings, and I was hoping to do it incrementally, with a lot less money on the line, in case I screwed up. The total number of units would require an investment of $3.2 million, and the bank was only prepared to lend me 70 percent of the total cost. That meant that of the $10,000 I had budgeted for each unit, I would now only have $7,000.

Too scared to be excited, I asked, "How about if I do it in two sections — one hundred sixty at a time?" My banker surprised me by saying, "Okay. I know it's your first project. I can go along with that." So I got the commitment for the entire cost of construction — $2.240 million, broken down as $7,000 a unit. In the end, we came in on budget. This meant I didn't have to use any of the Rausmans' money, but it also meant I would have to cut costs dramatically. When I spoke with Moses about the discrepancy, he just shrugged and said, "We can do that." And he showed me how it was done.

The Rausmans hired a young ordained rabbi from a New York City synagogue to work as our foreman. Sidney, who had prior experience home-building in Muncie, New York, arrived in his traditional black hat. I offered him $150 a week. He countered with $500. I countered his counter with the same $150. Finally, he said, "Tell you what — I'll work for you for six weeks, and after that time if you don't like my work, you can fire me without pay. But if you decide to keep me on, I get that $500 a week I deserve." That sounded reasonable enough, so I agreed to his terms. By the time those arduous six trial weeks were behind us, Sidney had earned my respect. He not only got his pay raise but he remained in my employ until 1974 — eleven years later. During that period, as a member of the clergy, he performed a wedding ceremony for my mother-in-law. He also divorced his devoutly religious wife and married a *shiksa* from Las Vegas, who converted to Judaism and remained with him until his death. The reason our relationship eventually came to an end was his betrayal of me, which I will discuss in a later chapter. At the time we parted, he owned 30 percent of my business. He must have thought, however wrongly, that 30 percent wasn't enough.

In those early days of my fledgling career, Sidney was of great value helping me deal with red tape, hiring and firing, and resolving problems with the production team. What I learned over the course of this undertaking was that, if you don't know the answer to something, hire or partner with someone who does. It's also imperative that he or she be someone you have reason to trust. Without a credible referral, you may have to go with your gut — and your gut is not always the best barometer.

A highly experienced general contractor will mastermind the project for you and know how to run the operation from beginning to end. They are acquainted with all the people in the county worth knowing, and where to find the right materials and peoplepower at the best possible prices — and under precisely the right conditions. They are also familiar with local real estate laws, and charged with hiring a reliable construction team. The more experienced the contractor, the cheaper, in general, will be the overall building costs. Sidney was not a general contractor, but he knew a number of ways for saving money. First, he hired the black bricklayers from a southern region of Virginia, who were glad for the work and willingly slept in the basement, which was the only available space. Then he hired the concrete team from Italy. After that came the mainframe workers from Norway, who were used to constructing in wood. No matter the season — blazing hot or freezing cold — those hearty Scandinavians wore nothing but swim shorts every day, and sang in their native Norwegian as they worked. They also charged us much less and did a better job than their American equivalents. This was their expertise, and they were duly proud of their skills. The Norwegians were considered better than the Swedes, who were known for their excessive pride and for putting too high a price on their handiwork. The electrician was an American — an Orthodox Jew with side curls. Despite the number of kids he had to support — an even dozen — he charged much less than the average electrician with far fewer mouths to feed.

Once our discounted, but highly skilled and motivated, workers began construction on the units, they were far enough along after four months that, even without the roofing in place, we were able to rent the first ninety apartments over the course of a single weekend. Then we began to build the second section of units across the street. Along the way, we constructed a retaining wall to block the incinerator from view and then used its ashes as filler for the uneven ground on which we erected the buildings. A layer of grass completed the cover-up, and no one suspected what was buried beneath. We also compensated the single-family homeowners with that fraction of an acre we had promised them.

Not only did we come in on budget, we had also built a lovely home for my family at no extra charge. It had occurred to me in the beginning that I was now in a position to offer a number of building contractors a hefty infusion to their bottom line over the next couple of years. Why would they not be willing to reward me with a small perk that would add little more than two percent to their respective costs and yet instill a strong feeling of good will between us — perhaps for future projects? My instincts were right. Every one of them was willing to oblige. So over the next couple of years, as the units were being built from the foundation up, so was the Bash family home on the two lots I owned on the upscale street of Yates Boulevard. By the time the project was finished, I had a

5,000-square-foot house, almost $750,000 in cash, and half-interest in an enterprise that eventually yielded me another $1 million in profit. For the new kid on the block, I had far exceeded my expectations. Eventually, some of my neighbors were impressed enough by my work that they chose to invest in my projects.

Everyone affected by this venture received their share of benefits, but no one more so than I. It was official. I was a real estate entrepreneur.

 convivio

As a prime example of how wrong bankers can be in predicting trends, over the next fifteen years I would build 6,000 apartment units across New York State — from Albany in the north to New York City in the south, 2,000 in Dutchess County alone. After a while, I no longer required bank money to get my loans. Private investors were so confident in my ability to deliver them a profit that they rarely hesitated to become involved. In one case a banker gave me a $100,000 loan in exchange for my signature on a promissory note. He based his decision solely on the fact that he liked me. That was a lot of money to be lending back then, equivalent to $1 million in today's deflated currency. And every one of those 1963 dollars was based on solid trust.

A Matter of Race

After I began leasing the apartments, a prospective tenant arrived one day and stood apart from the others. In a time when racial discrimination was still tacitly acceptable, even in the more tolerant North, every tenant to whom I had rented thus far was a member of the white majority. That was not the case with this young gentleman, who inquired about a lease and forced me into the uncomfortable task of turning him down. Then, having set me up beforehand, he reported the matter to human rights authorities who, in turn, forced me to defend myself.

Sitting across the desk from the government agent in charge of the case, I was roundly condemned for my alleged discrimination. The man said, "You're from Israel, so you know what it's like to be the object of bigotry. How can you refuse to rent to anyone based on his skin color?"

I told him, "I'm a businessman, and you know as well as I that were I to rent to a black family, I would not be able to rent to anyone else. It's an unfortunate fact of life, and I feel terrible about it, but we all have to make a living."

I did promise him that once I had rented the majority of units, I would encourage black families to move in. And, when the time came, I kept that promise. In the end, we had successfully integrated about a dozen black families into the units out of a total number of three hundred. When not one of the tenants complained about my new policy of integration, it became obvious that, however slowly, times and attitudes were finally changing.

After leasing every available unit, my job was done and it was time to move on. Using my winning formula, I bought out the land across the road and built another forty buildings.

The new project involved the Rausman brothers and other members of their Orthodox community, some of whom were immigrants from Belarus, like Joseph Kushner. These were men with a highly developed survival instinct that, having helped them endure the Holocaust, was now serving them well in peacetime.

Pretty Penny

One of my potential investors at that time was Abe Meltzer, who, without knowing me, drove in from Great Neck, Long Island — about ninety miles southeast of Poughkeepsie — to explore several properties with me. Afterward, we went to a restaurant, where he pulled a blank check out of his wallet, and signed it over to me, telling me to fill in any amount I wanted. I told him I needed between $500,000 and $600,000, but passed the check back to him. "I don't do business this way," I said. "If you're serious about investing with me, first prepare the papers and let me know when they're ready for review."

Although Abe was impressed with my response, I was bamboozled by his offer. The man had just met me an hour before, and he said he was prepared to invest as much as $2 million with me. By the end of that day, with a better understanding of each other, we became partners on several of my properties.

The owner of the house at the corner of Route 9 at Beechwood came with an offer to sell. He called the place "Pretty Penny" because, as he said, it was a genuine "money pit." But despite all the money that had been thrown into this pit, in order for me to replace it with a luxury apartment building,

I had to tear it down to the ground. One morning days later, just as the bulldozer was moving toward its appointed target, I shouted out my second thoughts. "No! Stop! Don't! That house has value. Let's move it somewhere." So the moving bulldozer came to a halt, and Sidney and I came to an agreement. Rather than pay someone to trash it, we would move it to a lot we already owned a couple of blocks away, and then we would sell the house along with the lot as a package deal. Once we laid the foundation, we got the city to cut down overhead electrical wires, allowing our two trucks, each carrying half of the house, to make the two-block journey toward its new residence. The story made the Poughkeepsie newspapers, which included a photo of Sidney waving out of the second-floor window as the truck pulled away. Despite Pretty Penny's mounting expenses, we found a buyer and managed to make a decent profit. Beyond the monetary compensation, however, I felt good about saving the house — rezoning it for a brand new life.

On a different lot we owned nearby sat another empty house, which is where I moved my family while our own new home was being built, however slowly, by my team of contractors. It was while we were living there that daughter Sharon was born.

Other ventures followed. One of them, a single-family home, had an entry on Joel Place, which I had named for my second son. (That's one of the perks that come with real estate development. You sometimes get to name a street for someone you love.) Yigal was in charge of that project, where we built fifty to a hundred reasonably priced homes. For example, a lovely three-bedroom home went for $10,000, $2,000 of which was pure profit. These figures may not sound impressive in relation to today's currency. But this was the early 1960s, when you could dine in a fine restaurant for ten bucks, including tip, and buy a home for the same price we would pay these days for a well-trashed car.

I had come a long way in the past few years, from foreign-born college graduate to successful businessman with an impressive and growing résumé. And I was just getting started.

ॐॐॐ

Summing Up

Brand new to the business of land development, I had more than enough distractions to keep me from focusing on my chosen career, including a wife and family. What kept me moving productively forward was realizing that, aside from the will to work hard and the determination to succeed, I was able to draw upon the experiences of others to guide me along the path. I was also able to recognize an opportunity whenever it came my way and in whatever obscure form it arrived on scene. Of course, occasionally a good one slipped past me, but there is no way to have them all; nor should there be. I believe in leaving something for the other guy. There's usually enough to go around.

The 1958 building venture turned out to be an excellent starter project for me, not only because I began learning the power of rezoning (the leaky basement, remember?), but also because I acquired the perfect mentor in Charlie Patrick. Of course it also didn't hurt that my father was a builder in Israel and felt a paternal duty to share his wisdom and the benefit of his experience with me. And true, he managed to find me my first two investors. But it doesn't take a father with connections to get started in any business. What it takes is dogged persistence, belief in yourself, and, if possible, someone willing to mentor you.

As you already know, within five years of starting my real estate career, I took on the City Council of Poughkeepsie, New York, and a group of hostile homeowners to transform a flawed piece of property with a defunct incinerator into what would become two communities of three hundred twenty rental units, each within forty separate apartment buildings. And, even more incredible, I prevailed.

If you are interested in rezoning real estate to its full potential, follow my simple steps, or modify them to suit your needs:

1. Meet with the city's planning commission, and present your case. If you don't win their approval, the process ends right there. Or, at least until you regroup. But if you manage to gain their favor, next stop is your city council, which has the power to overrule the planning commission, along with your rezoning ordinance. So put on your best smile and focus your gaze on whoever around you is holding your attention. Your job is to convince them that their opinion matters to you.

2. With approval of the planning commission, meet at a public hearing with city council and as many members

of the community as are motivated to attend. The way the hierarchy works is, the closer a homeowner's residence to your site, the greater their leverage for objection and the more motivated you are to appease them. (See #3 below.)

3. Side bar: Prior to the city council hearing, find a way to meet with the more "persuadable" of the city's decision makers and make your case to win them over. This is where diplomacy comes in handy, as well as a sharp knowledge of how to play by the rules. As Charlie Patrick explained to me, there are certain officials you begin to recognize as receptive to a game of *quid pro quo*. But you have to play so subtly that none of the players needs acknowledge the game for what it is. Above all, it is up to you to demonstrate how valuable the project would be to the community — and, since this is essentially true, it could be all you need to win.

4. Rehearse your big performance. Charlie knew a couple of council members that fit into the persuadable category and he rehearsed the scenario with me that I would then play out with them. A few days later, we held our informal meeting, and it went just as Charlie predicted. We had persuaded them, and we won our case. Although the power of persuasion is not always as easy as it sounds in this situation, the more often you apply it, the easier and more natural it becomes. Here is where I retell the story, adding the crucial details. Pay close attention, as some day you may find yourself in a

similar scenario and you will want to prepare yourself accordingly. During the fateful meeting, as you already know, one of the council members made a point of admiring my London Fog raincoat, which I instinctively took off and handed to him as a "gift." He took it without hesitation, knowing he was expected to earn it. Clearly, he had done this sort of thing before. Another council member confided that the mayor — who was not present — had previously expressed an interest in owning a new color TV. I made a mental note to order one the following morning and have it delivered to his home. The trick was for both the mayor and the new owner of my London Fog to vote *against* me, which would eliminate any suspicion of foul play. I hoped they knew what they were doing in my behalf, but I reminded myself I was dealing with seasoned pros and that these were the rules of the game they had perfected long before I walked onto the scene.

5. Besides meeting with city officials, be sure to engage in shuttle diplomacy among community members and local stakeholders, particularly the most disgruntled of them. I won over a number of them with Charlie's classic method of WIIFM. Because it was an eyesore, I focused their attention on the ugly, non-functioning incinerator — object of everyone's scorn. This issue resonated particularly well with those residents living close enough to face it whenever they looked through their windows. And those were the votes I wanted. I introduced myself as the builder who would

camouflage the monstrosity by building a retaining wall to hide it from their otherwise pastoral view. If that wasn't enough to satisfy them, I was also prepared to add a fraction of an acre to each of their backyards. Where was the downside? From what they could see, none existed. I was now a folk hero to a precious few — come to liberate this lovely community from that unspeakable blot on their landscape. The rest, the unenlightened and/or more militant among them, were still hoping to overturn their planning commission's decision.

6. On the day of your city council hearing, be ready to defend yourself against an army of indignant residents. Out of the five voting members of the council, I had to depend on the numbers working in my favor. The mayor, as preplanned, cast his vote against me, as did the man in charge of that ward. But having adopted Charlie's power of persuasion, which I embellished with my own innate skills, I was ultimately able to make my case for community benefits and absence of environmental impact. In the end, I won over the council and was now eligible to apply for a construction loan. My victory did not endear me to the angry no-growth advocates. They hadn't liked me from the start, being an outsider — even a foreigner. But by now, their opinions no longer mattered to me. I had to focus on building the three hundred twenty units and the forty apartment buildings in which to house them.

To get maximum benefit from this first chapter, memorize the following capsulized version of your general plan and ingrain it into your brain for easy access. You will want to expand and/or modify it as you apply it to your specific circumstances.

- Choose a relatively small city directly in the path of growth.
- Meet with neighbors living adjacent to the property.
- Meet with each council member separately.
- Support council members during and between election cycles. Bribery not allowed.
- Before taking your first step, minimize the possibilities of making any of the three biggest mistakes in buying real estate: 1) the wrong property in the wrong location, 2) the wrong time in the market cycle, and 3) the wrong (i.e., inflated) price.

You are playing in the major leagues now, so it is essential to learn the strategies that separate you from the minors, including how to overcome objections.

ଌଌଌ

The secret of getting ahead is getting started.

~ Mark Twain

ଌଌଌ

CHAPTER 2

IN THE BEGINNING, THERE WAS THE VACANT LAND—AND THEN IT WAS REZONED 1931–1949

Every youth owes it to himself and to the world to make the most out of the stuff that is in him.

~ Orison Swett Marden

చించించి

Even as a toddler, I loved to examine and reimagine things. I would see items in store windows — watches, for example — which, if opportunity permitted, I would take apart, scrutinize, and then reassemble. It has been said often enough that it must be true: Look to your talents and passions as a child and you will begin to see the adult you will one day become. When you nurture your gifts along the way, they will shine a beacon into your future, directly to your heart's desire. My curiosity about how things worked and how I could improve them was the master link to my life's goal.

During my first eight years of formal education, because my father followed the Orthodox tradition, I attended a religious school in Jerusalem called Talmud Torah. My mother was Orthodox, too, but of the more modern variety, having grown up in the home of an ambassador, where many non-Jews came to visit. From the first grade on, I had a perfect report card — nothing but A's in all of my eighteen subjects, and I was considered the best of the entire student body. Along the way, I became editor of the school newspaper. I was a natural choice since I spoke not only fluent Hebrew and a little Arabic (because of our neighbors), but English, as well, which was mandatory in our school system, beginning with the fifth grade. My English teacher, Mr. Isby, was Australian. Each day he would come to class, sit down at his desk, and say something in his accented speech like, "I sit." Then he would stand up and say, "I stand." That was how he taught us the language, performing actions while explaining them in English. So, when I came to the United States, I was fairly proficient, especially with the written language. But when it was spoken too fast, as it tended to be in New York/New Jersey, I would get terminally lost in translation.

One day when I was thirteen my math teacher, a Frenchman whose last name was pronounced "Lulu" (probably with a different spelling), became inexplicably confused in class and was suddenly unable to teach. Seeing he was in trouble and feeling confident in my knowledge of the subject, I raised my hand and said, "Why don't you sit down, sir? I can teach the lesson." And he did. And *I* did. Prior to our graduation ceremony, where I was invited to speak to my fellow classmates, many of those in my math class wrote something like the following in my autograph book: "I will always remember the day you taught Mr. Lulu a few things about math ...." Fortunately, my overconfidence didn't affect my grade.

When I was ready for high school, my father insisted on sending me to another Orthodox school, but this time my mother resisted. "No! I want my son to learn from the best." She knew the top-rated high school in Israel was the one established by Hebrew University, and she was determined to send me there. My parents argued. My mother won. That meant I would attend a school with extremely high standards, where I would be competing with bona fide geniuses. For purposes of admittance, they checked my IQ at 155, the highest in the school. Then they tested my general knowledge by asking me a series of random questions, one of which referred to a sixteenth-century Portuguese Marrano Jew named Uriel Acosta. Fortunately, I just happened to know the answer. The professor who quizzed me was duly impressed. So, thanks in part to Señor Acosta, I was accepted by my mother's school of choice. However, I was not the only impressive student gaining admission. That meant that even as a straight-A pupil, I was no longer able to compete on the level I had in elementary school. My grade point average soon dipped to a B or B-. At one point, even a C. The news didn't sit well with my parents, nor did it with my sense of self-worth. So, I had to excel at something else. I had to rezone. Good thing, too, since, as you see, the process of rezoning shaped the course of my life.

In high school, I found what I was looking for with electronics, which was a natural fit for me and earned me a few points for my entrepreneurial spirit. Coincidentally, electronics was the latest trend in a world not yet widely introduced to the phenomenon of TV. In pre-Israel Jerusalem there was still only radio to entertain and inform us in our homes. So at age thirteen I decided to build a radio station, which I called The Voice of the Merry Student, and which I set up in a corner of my parents' spacious bedroom. By doing so, I immediately placed myself center stage among my classmates. Every day after school, my friends would come over, and we would perform music and skits on the air. With my resonant voice and exceptional command of the Hebrew language, I became the natural choice for announcer as well as the stand-up comic. (Well, it was *my* radio station.) And this was no amateur operation. Over the next four years, the broadcasts eventually reached out to every high school student in Jerusalem and Tel Aviv, and, in fact, the whole of Eretz Israel/Palestine. In the pursuit of exceptionalism in whatever area excited me, I had rezoned myself from a mere student to the owner and operator of a popular radio station. Not bad for a high school kid. Even my parents conceded the fact.

Up until then, commercials had never been aired on radio. Everything in the territory was government-controlled. But I changed that policy the day I walked into a record store and said to the owner, "Give me your records to play for free, and I'll advertise your store on my radio station." Understanding the inherent value to his business, the man agreed to the deal. So he gave me the records I required, which I would play a few times and then turn in for a new collection. In exchange, I produced and broadcast a commercial that promoted the store's merchandise and sale items, and made a point of informing listeners where they could purchase the recordings I had played.

Sure enough, I helped increase the store's sales and garnered the owner's trust. Our association continued for as long as I ran that station, as it was of mutual benefit. So not only did I rezone myself from student to entrepreneur, I also rezoned the record store to a higher level of success.

One of the things I did to amuse my friends at school was install a hidden recorder in our classroom closet. Whenever the teacher, Mr. Shapira, walked down the aisle between desks and stopped at a certain spot, the recorder would instantly activate and a loud voice, seemingly out of nowhere, was heard singing in florid Russian or some other exotic language. Befuddled, Mr. Shapira would invariably look in vain for the source, but always came up empty. Then, one day, when he opened the closet door, he spied the offending device and banished it from the room. It didn't take long to connect the dots, which led him straight to me.

I also had a black-and-white movie camera — something none of the other students owned at the time. So I was able to take candid shots of teachers in awkward positions and perform photo tricks for my highly receptive classmates. Years later, in planning our twenty-five-year class reunion, someone from the committee called from Israel to remind me to bring along those movies. During the event, we screened them five or six times, recalling how brashly we had interacted with our teachers — of course, in good-natured amusement. During the reunion program, my American wife, Arlene, who had no command of Hebrew, noticed one particular word that all of the speakers were using repeatedly: *Micha*. I laughed. "That's me they're talking about; Micha is Hebrew for Michael." Arlene was tickled to know that her husband was a legend among his classmates — if not for his knowledge of history or physics, at least for his wicked sense of humor.

So, I had become known for a number of things: My radio station, taking movies, that hidden recorder, and my offbeat brand of comedy. Whenever there was a party, I was the one to pick up on all the activities taking place, and then stand in front of the class and satirize them.

Having already served as the editor of my elementary school newspaper, it seemed logical that I write, as well. In Israel, there was a publication called *Sikot*, a humor magazine fashioned after England's famous *Punch*. Somehow I managed to convince the editors to publish a series of my humorous stories under the title "The Adventures of Benjamin."

But I was spreading myself thin. With too much to distract me during my senior year of high school, I had begun to slack off again on my studies. Math had always been my best subject, and now I was failing my tests. So, to bolster my grades, I was given a special tutor, a lovely young woman with fatally flawless legs that easily distracted me from learning the square root of anything. One afternoon, some friends and I had planned to get together and hang out, but my math lesson stood in the way. I told them of my dilemma. "I can't cancel my lesson. She'll tell my teacher."

They said, "Don't worry. We'll come in like we're from the Haganah, and we'll convince her we're on a mission."

So they dressed up like armed terrorists and entered the room, but before they could speak, my leggy tutor took one look at them, turned white, and fainted. Later, she complained to Mr. Shapira that I had used my friends to avoid my math lesson with her. That was the moment Mr. Shapira lost his temper, flew into a rage, and called in my parents. He said, "If you can do a terrible thing like this and scare a well-meaning young woman who is simply trying to teach you math, I would have no recourse but to dismiss you from school." Then he stopped and thought and changed his mind. "On the other hand … your teachers are proud of you and your high IQ. If we let you go, it would lower the school's excellent standards. So, okay … you may stay … but you have to agree to shape up." That was easy enough. I agreed to shape up.

In 1947, during my last semester, graduation came in April instead of June. The administration had shortened our school year by two months because the country wanted to recruit high school graduates into the army to fight for our independence. My knowledge of English was limited, and it was essential for me to pass the class in order to graduate. What did I do? Fortunately there was a beautiful girl named Aviva who sat next to me in class. Aviva was extremely friendly. She was also smart and willing to share her test answers with me. Problem solved. For our final exam, she got her well-deserved A, and I was thrilled to pass with an unearned B. Furthermore, Aviva had just done her country a service, allowing me to graduate and become eligible for military duty. For all she knew, she might have helped change the course of the war.

Months earlier, while I was still in high school, I had become involved with one of the most hard-fought and contentious rezonings of the twentieth century. Eretz Israel was marked throughout its history by alternating cycles of war and peace — arguably more war than peace — and a diverse population with ever-changing leadership and ever-shifting belief systems and customs.

The State of Israel Before It Was the State of Israel

I was born in Jerusalem in March 1931, where Jews, Christians, and Muslims lived together in relative harmony. That is, if you didn't count the ongoing uprisings by certain Arab groups or the oppressive rule of the British, who had controlled the region since the League of Nations handed it to them in 1922. After adding the area to their broadening realm following World War I, which was responsible for the crushing defeat of the Turks and the Ottoman Empire, the Brits had no intention of surrendering the land without a bloody battle. They were still the British Empire, after all.

The Jewish populace was able to count seven countries as enemies, with a total population of 40,000,000 — all of them attacking us simultaneously. By contrast, the area of Israel — known as the British Empire's Palestine Mandate — had a population of about 500,000, with a ratio of 80:1. Enemy countries included Syria, Lebanon, Egypt, Saudi Arabia, and Jordan. Because the Jordanian army was trained by the Brits, in combat they resembled the British army, which only added to the complications.

Discontented with the status quo and the ongoing Arab conflicts, the regional Jews rose against their oppressors by way of three distinct Zionist underground organizations. The Stern Group under the leadership of Yitzhak Shamir (future prime minister of the State of Israel) was the most violent of the terror organizations, even with its small membership of two hundred. Led by another eventual prime minister, Menachem Begin, the Irgun was responsible for, among other notable incidents, the 1946 bombing of the legendary King David Hotel. The Irgun had planned to blow up the British administrative offices located in one of the hotel's wings, but the damage spread throughout much of the building, resulting in forty-six injuries and the death of ninety-one people of various nationalities. The Haganah, whose primary purpose was Jewish statehood, was a government-sanctioned paramilitary group headed by David Ben-Gurion, the man who would become Israel's first prime minister. Because the country had been armed by multiple nations, each manufacturing its own weapons, my contemporaries and I were trained from age thirteen to shoot with twenty-five varieties of guns, including a Belgian Parabellum, a German Mauser, an Italian Pistola Barretta, and an American Colt .45. My skills with a gun, any gun, served me well from the day I joined the underground.

While I was serving, I began a new radio station, which I called The Voice of the Merry Soldier. At that time, Israel had no organized communications companies. It was like the Wild West, where, since there were no rules, you were free to set your own. This was something like the internet was to become decades later. Our announcer, Eliezar Schmuelli, and I wrote a hymn, which we played at the beginning of every broadcast. One day the Haganah's transmitter broke down and they asked to use mine so they could warn the public of an imminent attack. In order to stay one step ahead of the British at all times, the Haganah would transmit messages from different locations every ten minutes. I was happy and honored to oblige.

My father was a rich man, and he supported the Haganah. People came from Begin's group for equal support, but he turned them down. They did not take his rebuff kindly, and threatened him. One day in 1946, when I was fifteen, I was sitting at home near a window, and spotted two armed men running after him. They struck my dad on the head with the butt of their guns and, by the time I reached him, he was on the ground with an open injury to his scalp. With the help of a friend, I managed to get him safely inside the house. But we couldn't take him to the hospital because it was controlled by the British, and we would never let them know about the internal fighting. Instead, we brought in a Jewish doctor to treat him at home until he recovered, which took about a month, although the scar on his head remained a permanent memento. After that incident the Haganah posted two guards inside our house to protect my father day and night. Every time I came home I would see those two men sitting in the living room playing cards or chess, or just reading. Despite their seeming detachment, they were always on the alert, always ready to defend their own.

That wasn't the last time we had a brush with disaster. One day, close to our home, the Irgun ambushed a British convoy and placed a bomb under one of their vehicles. In response, the British started shooting in every direction. My mother was in the kitchen at the time, and fell to the floor for safety. Bullets came bursting through the window as I rushed to her aid. During the latter days of my childhood, this is how we spent much of our lives: defending ourselves against attacks, retaliating for attacks, initiating attacks, and dodging attacks. But because it was the only lifestyle I knew, I assumed it was normal.

Moshe was my best friend at school, and because he was well-spoken, he was appointed announcer for one of Irgun's transmitters. After the war, he would become a purser for El Al Airlines, in charge of the flight attendants. Because he was exceptionally good-looking, the women were delighted to have him around. When he was best man at my wedding, all the eligible females in attendance, including my sister-in-law, spent the entire event in fruitless pursuit of his favor. When Moshe finally settled down with a wife, it was with a traditional Israeli who eventually bore him four children.

Rigorous training for the Haganah took place in the basement of a large grade school on Jaffa Road in Jerusalem, which belonged to the Alliance organization from France. One day I was put in charge of watching the gate. Should anyone from the British army come by, it was my job to push a button and alert everyone to hide the weapons. One evening at ten o'clock, I was standing alone when I felt the cold metal of a gun barrel press against my neck. I spun around and my eyes locked on a young man and woman, who asked me in clipped English, "What are you doing here?"

I gave them the first excuse that came to mind. "Well, I met this girl, and she said she would meet me here ... and ...."

They followed with a battery of miscellaneous questions, testing my trustworthiness, and finally said, "Okay, you can relax. You passed. We're Jewish, too. We're British."

I breathed a sigh of relief.

As the result of military training, I was in prime physical condition. And how could I not be? We would regularly walk the fifty-mile journey from Jerusalem to the northern part of the Galilee. Along the way, as part of our endurance exercises, we hiked three round trips up and down Mount Tabor in the Jezreel Valley, where Jesus is said to have met with Elijah. Fighting was also part of the discipline. I learned how to box and to fight with a club. One day when I was club-fighting with a friend, Mordecai Tamari, I accidentally hit him squarely in the head, causing his scalp to bleed profusely. We immediately took him to the hospital, where he got excellent care. Fortunately, there were no repercussions. Twenty-five years later I encountered Mordecai at our class reunion, and he reminded me, somewhat good-naturedly, that I had almost killed him that day in training. Instinctively, I recruited my fists to demonstrate where he had fallen short in his technique. "Look, you're supposed to punch like this ... not like *this*." Not surprisingly, he turned down my offer for a rematch.

Traveling from Tel Aviv to Jerusalem was also fraught with danger. On one occasion the Arabs staged a bloody ambush in an area called Bab-el-Wad, where they killed a great many people and destroyed a number of cars. In commemoration of that tragic event, monuments composed of debris from those cars were installed along the road to Jerusalem.

Another day, my friend Judah and I were returning to Jerusalem from the front lines. We got off the bus at the same stop. I walked to the right on my way home, and he went to the left. Just as he turned, Judah was hit by shrapnel and died on the spot. After that horrific incident, whenever I saw his grieving father walking along the street, I would cross to the other side — survivor's guilt overwhelming me. Another friend, Uri Kaduri, met with a similar fate one day when he was out on the street and caught a stray bullet. With the Arabs shelling the city so frequently, I began to feel safer at the front lines with my soldier friends than I did back home in Jerusalem. Whenever the air raids came, everyone in the family would rush into the shelter, except for my father. A self-professed *shtarker* (strong person), he refused to be bullied, no matter how potentially perilous the circumstances. As his nearly grown son, I felt obligated to stay behind with him. My reasoning was that if he could handle it, so could I. But my father, who had a lifelong habit of hedging his bets, usually took precautions. As a safety measure against such attacks, he would place one bed on top of another so that, should a bomb drop while he was sleeping, he had a good chance of surviving a direct hit. A bit more of a risk taker than he, I slept with no overhead protection. Fortunately, neither of our viewpoints was put to the test.

In April 1948, after leaving the underground, I joined the army. It was just one month before the War of Independence began and I was defending the Church of Notre Dame, situated across from the walls of the Old City. The French church was residence to a number of nuns, who were raped by the incoming Arabs. I was among a company of soldiers dispatched to the church to protect the holy sisters.

In contrast to the large number of German guns in the hands of the Arabs, our arsenal was limited. But we devised a clever plan to compensate for the shortage. In every second window of the church we placed a gun, and, in the alternates, we installed a pipe — so that from a short distance away, it appeared we had double the number of guns we actually possessed. Once combat began, we would shoot out of one window and then rush to the next and shoot from there, and so on. The Arabs never caught on. Nor did they take note of the perils presented by their traditional white headdresses, which, during nighttime attacks, made them easy targets. Once we had killed a few of them, a few others would run away, giving us a chance to pursue them and confiscate their guns. Using that strategy, every night we were attacked we managed to build up our arsenal of Czechoslovakian MG-34s machine guns. On one occasion, our army intercepted an Arab boat en route to its destination, giving us still more weaponry to stockpile. Ironically, the longer the conflict lasted, the better we were weaponized.

Located fifteen miles from Jerusalem, the United Nations-controlled Mount Scopus was home to Hebrew University and the largest Hadassah Hospital in the country. An adjacent mountain was under Arab control, which made access to Mount Scopus fraught with risk. Every three months a contingent of 120 civilians and policemen was permitted entry to oversee matters related to the two institutions. A biblical zoo was also located up there, but with no proper staff to care for the starving animals. One particularly weak lion lay constantly on his side with a belly so empty it stuck to his back. Inspired by the tragedy of his plight, I wrote a ballad dedicated to him. After the 1967 war Israel regained control of the mountain, and all the animals were sent to the biblical zoo in Jerusalem, where they were given the best care. I was glad to see the starving lion among them. With all odds against him, he had somehow managed to survive. Not unlike the State of Israel.

Until now, the army had no radio communication with Mount Scopus, which they needed desperately. General Moshe Dayan knew about my radio station and instructed me to create one that would provide them contact with the university and hospital. One day, Dayan picked me up in his car and, along the way, stopped at a grape orchard. Not one to ask or even need permission for such things, he spontaneously climbed over the fence, picked a large bunch of grapes, and shared them with me. Dayan loved people, and the feeling was mutual, but, as with many great heroes, he had trouble with women. After losing an eye during a battle with the French in 1941, he began wearing a black patch. What became his signature accessory only added to his mystique and his undeniable sex appeal.

On the day I went to Mount Scopus to build Dayan's transmitter, I hid my secret plan inside my socks to avoid detection by the Arab Legion. The Arabs were frisking everyone in the area for weapons, but had neglected to order inspection of shoes — a lucky break for me. As soon as I arrived at the top of the mountain, I rushed to the basement of Hebrew University, where, just as I had anticipated, there were labs and electronics equipment to help me create the device. Within two days, I was able to communicate with Jerusalem. They were so happy to hear from me they wanted to reciprocate the favor. "What can we do for you?" they asked.

I said, "I want to talk to my mom."

Within the hour, a Jeep arrived at my mom's house and drove her and my youngest sister to the front lines. Bursting with pride, Mom called me from their military equipment. For a long time thereafter, I could do no wrong.

That first day my transmitter went into operation, one of the soldiers broadcast a popular song to the entire nation of Israel. Written by one of our most famous songwriters, Avigdor Hameiri, it could not have been more relevant to the moment. "From the Heights of Mount Scopus … I will bow to you, Jerusalem … and I always longed for you …."

A few days later I picked up the phone and overheard voices from the UN line speaking in Arabic at an unintelligible volume. Obviously, some kind of malfunction inside the switchboard made it possible to hear external conversations. I immediately called Jerusalem, amplified the sound to a level at which the reception was clear, and asked the military to send some agents to come listen and translate what they heard. I thought maybe we could gain some vital information. So a few days later two Mossad agents showed up at our headquarters. They listened in on the Arab/UN line and said, "Fabulous.

They're revealing everything about their movements, and we can hear and understand everything they say."

The agents interpreted all the instructions coming from the Arab army, describing the locations of their posts, how much ammunition they had — everything confidential that they needed to convey to their own military but avoid exposing to us. Based on that information, our translators were able to draw a detailed map, so that when Israel attacked those Arab sites, which they did years later, they knew where everything was situated and the kind and amount of weaponry they had. Ironically, that phone line remained open to our agents for the next eighteen years — until the 1967 Six-Day War. I have no doubt it helped lead us to victory.

Being stationed on Mount Scopus with its 2,700 feet of elevation and frequently freezing temperatures, we were periodically allowed delivery of oil to heat our living quarters at Hadassah Hospital. One day, we used that permission as a ruse to deliver ammunition, as well. I was disguised in a police uniform but because of the ample size of my head, no one could find a hat to fit me properly. So, when our bus went through inspection, the Arab in charge asked me what was wrong with the hat I was wearing. Without hesitation, I told him I was in such a rush that I had taken my friend's hat by mistake. He bought my excuse. By now I had learned that you had to think on your feet or it could cost you your life.

We had managed to hide the munitions we were carrying by placing a cylinder under an opening in the oil tanker. Then we filled it with oil, and closed and sealed it. When the Arabs checked the tanker, they used a measuring stick to confirm the presence of oil, and were satisfied with what they found. On the road to the hospital, our bus followed behind the tanker truck. Eventually, both vehicles had to turn left, but the over-burdened truck, which was going too fast, made a quick left in front of us and promptly toppled over on its side. Onlookers rushed to help, including members of the UN, but since we were naturally concerned they might find out what we were doing, we graciously declined, saying we could handle the situation ourselves. After the Arabs and the UN left, we turned the truck back upright and opened the secret door. Then we moved all the ammunition into the hospital basement, which was filled with medical supplies and related equipment. Once the grueling task was behind us, we inhaled deeply for the first time in hours and reveled in our clandestine victory.

I was on Mount Scopus for about 120 days. When I finally came back down the mountain, my hair was long — *like Moses descending from Mount Sinai*, I thought to myself with a grin. And aside from the few times I glimpsed through a telescope to gaze upon the female population of Jerusalem, I hadn't seen a woman for four months. During the time we were up there, we ate only the food we had brought with us. But due to my weakness for chocolate and the deprivation I was experiencing from doing without, I felt compelled to ask the food supplier if he had any in stock. When he said no, I naturally believed him — until one day I caught him biting into a half-eaten Hershey bar. I said, "Well, well, well … I would swear that's chocolate you've got there."

Embarrassed from having been caught in the act, he said, "If you promise not to tell anyone, I'll see that you have chocolates every day from now on ... without fail." That seemed like a fair bargain to me and my sweet tooth, so we both agreed to keep the man's secret in exchange for our daily supply.

Once Eretz Israel transformed into the State of Israel, it was organized enough to shut down my radio station and take over the state-sponsored Voice of Israel, which exists to this day, somewhat on a par with our own Voice of America. When I became a civilian again, I created my third and last radio station, which I called The Voice of the Merry Jamaha (Arabic for "friends"). I operated that for about a year — not for profit, but for pleasure. Then I shut it down to concentrate on my college career. Because of the three stations I had run as a kid, my story was accorded an article in the *Jerusalem Post*.

Now that I was home again, Grandfather ("Saba" in Hebrew) asked me to come and work for him, which I did — for the entire last year I remained in Israel, while also attending Hebrew University. At first I asked, "How much will you pay me?"

He opened the cash register drawer and said, "Take as much as you want. Don't worry about it."

I didn't abuse his generous offer. I took only what I needed.

Emigration, Education, and Engagement

Now it was 1950 and I was laser-focused on my education in electronics. There was only one appropriate school in Israel. But it was new, and there was no way yet of knowing how good it was. My natural second choice was to find an outstanding school in the United States, which was, and still is, the most advanced country on the planet in the field of electronics. I related my ambitions to my uncle in Newark, New Jersey, and he recommended the Newark College of Engineering, which would eventually become the prestigious New Jersey Institute of Technology. Even then, its stellar reputation was somewhere on a par with MIT or Cal Tech. Through my uncle, I submitted an application, and was immediately accepted based on my straight-A grade point average. (Well, almost straight-A. There was that iffy B in English I was forced to live down.) My intention was to study four years in the United States, graduate from college, and then return to Israel, where I would pursue a career in broadcasting.

My plan was to help pioneer Israel's television industry, which was just beginning to hint at its phenomenal future. But that, as you already know, is not what happened. Oh, I did go to the United States the following year, 1951, and I did graduate from the Newark College of Engineering. But the remainder of my plan was substantially rezoned along the way. The unexpected shift in my agenda might have been influenced, at least in part, by my meeting Arlene, who would not have transplanted well to the more rugged lifestyle of the young State of Israel. And pursuing broadcasting in the United States, where the industry was already well established, would not have been as groundbreaking an adventure as it would have been back home.

Attending school in the United States required me to improve my English in a hurry. It helped that I joined a national fraternity (Tau Epsilon Phi), became its local chaplain, and edited its newsletter. By my junior year I had met a fellow student in my English class, a beautiful Irish Catholic blonde named Arlene Sayers, and I longed for a way to attract her attention. Then our teacher gave us an assignment to stand in front of the room and sell something to the rest of the class, whatever product we had in mind. Hoping to take advantage of this assignment to win Arlene over, I came up with a unique idea. The first thing I did was approach three students who agreed to participate in the assignment, one of whom was Arlene.

The student presenting before me was selling a radio set. Another was selling a camera. By contrast, my own pitch would involve a lot more imagination. When it was my turn, I announced that I wasn't an ordinary salesman, that the things I sold were intangible: wisdom, friendship, and beauty. To represent wisdom, I called upon the first of my participants, a kid named Schnitzer, who also happened to be the smartest kid in school. As rehearsed, Schnitzer held up a slide rule as he walked to the front of the class and stood at attention next to me. In my sales pitch for wisdom, I explained its inherent value, along with the need for a good education and a thirst for knowledge. For friendship, there was a guy named George Siwolop from Ukraine (which was still part of the USSR and engaged in a Cold War with the U.S.). George came to the front of the class and extended his hand to me in friendship. In turn, I pointed out the benefits of friendly relations with other countries. And for beauty, I called upon the divine Arlene. Naturally, I had left her for last so I could spend more time with her. To the class, I cited the beauty of Arlene's lustrous blonde hair and various other parts of her anatomy — all in good taste, of course. She was melting in response to the flattery, and, just like that, I had sold Arlene on the benefits of my friendship.

Arlene lived just down the shore in Asbury Park, and from that day on I would carry her books for her after school — all the way to the train station. In the process, our friendship quickly advanced. We were now spending our daily lunch breaks at the fraternity house satisfying our mutual appetite for sex. When some of the members found out what we were doing at the same time they were conducting themselves so appropriately on campus, they called a meeting to consider their options. But, as it turned out, the guys objecting to my sex life were in the minority. The rest had no problem with however anyone spent his lunch hours — in or out of the frat house. They were not only trying to protect me, after all, but also themselves.

Arlene and I went together for our entire junior year and halfway through our senior year. Finally, one day she invited me to her parents' house, and I gladly accepted. I was determined to make a good impression. But when they picked me up at the train station, her father wasted no time in launching his inquisition, designed to take me down in a hurry. He said, "Your name is Michael, isn't it? We're Irish here, Michael, and Michael is an Irish name. Are you Irish?"

I said, "No. I come from Israel."

Dead silence. Then Arlene's mother spoke up. "Why did you Jews kill Jesus Christ?"

Shocked by her unbridled bigotry, all I could manage was, "That was 2,000 years ago. So, I don't know. I wasn't there."

After more dead silence, her father spoke between clenched teeth. "I'm taking you back to the station."

And he did, in record time. I had failed the boyfriend test, based solely on my DNA and on traditional church doctrine. Arlene's parents made it clear they had no intention of allowing their daughter to fraternize — or, God forbid, worse — with a Christ-killer. But Arlene was a healthy young girl, and she would not be discouraged. When summer came, I would travel to Asbury Park on weekends, rent a cheap hotel room, and wait for her to make her usual excuse to her parents, that she was going to the ocean to swim — when, in fact, she was on her way to my hotel room to engage her Christ-killer in sinful sexual intercourse.

Eventually she said to me, "I want to go to the synagogue with you."

I said, "Why?"

Extraordinarily candid, she said, "Because I want you to come to church with me. I want you to convert to Catholicism. Then my parents will accept you."

I told her there wasn't even the remotest chance of that happening — not with my strong Jewish heritage. And that was the day we broke up. I felt bad about it, but I was twenty-one. Eventually my broken heart mended. It took a few days.

Shortly thereafter, in 1955, I graduated from college, and immediately got an engineering job with Weston Electrical Instrument Company in Newark. I quickly found out that all my new colleagues were getting a starting salary of $100 a week. Mine was only $80, they told me, because I was not a U.S. citizen. That sort of workplace discrimination would not likely stand today, but I didn't mind at the time because I knew I would be good at my job and eventually surpass everyone else. I was right. Within a year I was making $250 a week and my American-born colleagues were making somewhere between $120 and $150. So, already, I was succeeding at the career for which I had been trained. Now it was time to think about how to use my established skills to rezone myself to a higher level — somewhere I would shine the brightest and where I would find the greatest satisfaction. Focused on invention and innovation, I created several devices, including the revolutionary controller that grew Weston Electrical's profits an extra $40 million a year. By contrast, it gave me, its inventor, a pathetic raise of $10,000 with no rights to the patent. But I can thank Weston's ingratitude toward me for my growing discontentment, and for ultimately motivating me to move on to greener pastures.

What Father had advised me was now resonating strongly. "As long as you work for other people, you'll never get anywhere." My father was speaking from a lifetime of personal experience. He owned and operated a hardware store and also built multiple-family dwellings — small apartment houses: four-family, eight-family, up to twenty-four family units in one building. I liked the idea a lot and figured this was how I would get into real estate. So I rezoned myself from full-time engineer into a hyphenate engineer-home builder. I was not yet ready to take on the heavier mantle of real estate developer, but I had taken the crucial first step.

After purchasing a parcel of land in 1958, I planned to develop it into lots for single-family homes. For the next two years I worked eight-hour days, five days a week, as an engineer. At the end of each workday, I would go to my site with my foreman, who constructed the houses for me. In the meantime, I was learning how to build cheaper — and still cheaper. The post-war real estate boom was tapering off, but my building career was just catching fire. Developing single-family homes made me good money, but not as much as the multi-unit apartment structures next on my agenda. Later on, there would be shopping centers, too, which would bring me the greatest profits of all. So I was always rezoning myself upward, and, as a result, increasing my profit. It helped considerably that I had found a knowledgeable and congenial mentor. Not everyone gets so lucky — which means you may have to work harder than I did to find a Charlie Patrick of your own. But it is assuring to know there are always people out there willing to help. The trick is to seek them out, to establish a bond with them, and to earn their trust. There should be something in it for them, too. You just have to find out what that "something" might be.

In 1960, I was able to fulfill the promise I had made to myself after feeling unappreciated at Weston — that as soon as I was making as much money at land development as I was at engineering, I would quit the engineering job and concentrate on the land. Three years later, in 1963, I did my first big rezoning and made my first million dollars.

Family Matters

To better understand the way my brain works, it might be helpful to know something about my ancestry. My grandmother died in childbirth, so my mother grew up without a mother of her own. Fortunately, her sister, Rivkah, who was about fifteen years older, became her surrogate parent. Eventually Aunt Rivkah married Mordecai Caspi, a distinguished businessman who ran the Israeli branch of Secocione Generale, a big Italian insurance company with headquarters on Jaffa Road. Eventually Uncle Mordecai was appointed Israeli ambassador to Latvia, Estonia, and Lithuania — three Baltic countries that gained their independence from Russia in the aftermath of World War II.

Because of Rivkah's marriage to Uncle Mordecai, my mother grew up in a wealthy section of Jerusalem called Talpiot. Their palatial home, with its lush carpeting and fine paintings and statuary, was as sumptuous as any Hollywood movie set.

By the time my mother reached the age of twenty-seven, she had had only one serious relationship with a man. Since most of her contemporaries were getting married in their late teens and early twenties, Aunt Rivkah and Uncle Mordecai were worried about her finding a husband. But they didn't have to worry any longer because that was the year she met my father, who was only about twenty and from a poor Chasidic family. He was also a gold-digger — unashamedly looking to marry a woman from a prosperous family, who could give him a proper start in life. Hoping to encourage their relationship despite his lack of credentials, my aunt and uncle promised Father that if he married their daughter they would give him a *nedoonia* (dowry) of £200. Father had no problem with such an arrangement. In fact he welcomed it, and he was fully prepared to earn his keep. When courting my mother, she later told me, he treated her with kindness and respect. Frequently he would take her to the park, where, knowing she liked to perch on a big rock, he predictably spread out his handkerchief for her to sit on. After they were married, Father kept his word to my uncle. He used the dowry money to open a store on Jerusalem's main street, where he sold building materials and eventually hired his younger brothers to work for him. Although he never attended college, Father had graduated from a *yeshivah* — a house of learning. He was self-taught and smart, and spoke several languages. As his business began to prosper, he opened another location in Tel Aviv and began venturing into real estate. In Jerusalem, he eventually built an entire street of apartment houses he called Meir Apartments, which he immodestly named for himself.

My parents were never a good match. Because of their widely diverse backgrounds and temperaments, they rarely spent a day without fighting. Yet, as hostile as their relationship became, they never broke up because divorce in their society was considered unacceptable. Conveniently, they found a way to relieve their frustrations, using me as a sounding board through which to complain about the other. I felt bad for my mother, who was a sensitive woman and had little sympathy for my father, who was crude and abusive. Not only did he beat my mother during her pregnancy with me, hitting her hard in the belly, he continued striking her throughout my childhood. He also thrashed my younger brother, Yigal, and me whenever he felt motivated, although Mother would try to stop him. Fortunately, his violent behavior came to a sudden halt one day after I picked up a can of food and threw it at him. His volatile temperament aside, Father took good care of me, sent me to college in the United States, and made sure I got a monthly check for my expenses. Later on, he confessed he regretted sending me away to college, because it took me permanently away from him. And since Yigal and he did not get along, he was left with no one to whom he could leave the family business. Eventually, Yigal attended college in the United States, as well, and achieved a Master's degree in physics. But, he, too, went into real estate — working with me for twenty years before feeling confident enough to go out on his own. Eventually he moved with his family to Houston, Texas, where he lived out a happy, fulfilling life.

My grandfather was a short man with a raspy voice. Born in Warsaw, Poland, the youngest of eight children, mostly boys, he graduated from college with a major in chemistry. He was also a Talmudic scholar, and studied every day. Once Hitler took control in Germany, Grandfather sensed the Nazi dictator would eventually come after the Jews, so he left his family behind and moved to Eretz Israel. As his predictions about Hitler began coming true, Grandfather sent his son, Shalom, back to Poland, hoping the evidence was now sufficient enough to convince his family of the imminent danger. But he made one tactical mistake. Shalom, as well as his other children, had all adapted a modern lifestyle, whereas the family in Poland was still steeped in the Orthodox tradition. Men wore the traditional black suits, black hats, and white shirts, as well as *payot* (sidelocks) and prayer shawls. Sending this modern young man, who, by contrast, was accused of dressing like "a goy," to come and lure the family away from their roots only made them more resistant. They were determined not to become secular like Grandfather's family had done, and if that was what it required of them to live in Israel, they would remain behind in Poland. Sadly, their stubbornness turned out to be their fatal flaw, and inadvertently condemned them to death. With one exception, the entire family was wiped out by the Nazis. And that one "exception," who had been wise enough to foresee the inevitable early enough, found a way to avoid capture. In the end, aside from Yigal, with whom he was not close, I was Grandfather's only grandchild, and we treasured the bond between us.

Soon after arriving in Eretz Israel, Grandfather met my grandmother, a beautiful young woman who worked at her family-owned hotel in Hebron. Once they married, Grandfather opened and operated a kitchenware store in Jerusalem. In the back of the shop, he installed a chemistry lab, where he produced a variety of goods with ingredients imported from a number of countries, even Germany. One of the more popular

of his products was black hair dye. He also made an insecti-
cide called Flit and sold Borax as a strong alternative to laundry detergent. Also, he made keys and locks for his customers.
In my own corner of the lab, Grandfather taught me to perform a number of chemical experiments, including gold and
silver plating, which required the application of acid to steel,
brass, or copper. Whatever items I made, such as gold keys, I
gave away as presents. It wasn't difficult to get the materials
I needed. I would simply accompany a friend to the lab at
Hebrew University and rummage through their garbage. Some
of the things I retrieved might have been dangerous, even poisonous, but my friend and I were familiar enough with their
properties to feel safe in handling them.

Because Grandfather was the only businessman in the city,
possibly the entire country, with access to his unique product
line, he became highly successful. In addition, people would
go to his store to tap into his broad knowledge of the Talmud.

Talmudic Wisdom

One of my favorite stories from the Talmud centers on a rabbi
named Meir, who held one strong opinion on a particular
topic, while all his fellow rabbis held another. Determined to
win the heated argument, he said, "You see that tree out there?
If I'm right, it will uproot itself from the ground and move a
hundred feet away ... and then stop." Sure enough, the tree
moved a hundred feet. Everyone shrugged it off, claiming the
rabbi was using magic to make his case. But he persisted. He
said, "If I'm right ... you see the walls of this temple? The walls

will move forty-five degrees." Again, he was right. The walls moved exactly forty-five degrees. And yet the other rabbis continued to insist it was they who were right. Finally, Rabbi Meir said, "Okay, still not convinced? Well, then ... if I'm right, God Himself will come and assure you that I'm right."

All of a sudden, a booming voice was heard from heaven. It said, "Listen to my son, Meir. He is correct."

Still unwilling to yield, the other rabbis scrambled to find that place in the Torah that would support their position. Finally, one of them read from the definitive passage, which clearly concluded that regardless of laws — in all cases and without exception — the majority wins. "And we are the majority," the rabbis said, feeling vindicated.

According to unofficial sources, after Rabbi Meir lost his argument, he also lost his mind, as well as his faith. Grandfather told me that story to prove a point. The law is the law, according to the Bible, but the will of the majority supersedes the law. That landmark conclusion, written over 3,000 years ago, may well have ignited the first spark of democracy in the world. Grandfather also taught me about the thirty-six righteous people from each generation who inhabit the earth — and who are considered the basis for our existence. Were there only thirty-four or thirty-five of these righteous individuals, according to this principle, the earth's population would be reduced to zero. These unidentified people are called *lamed vavniks*. Could you or I be one of them? Only God knows.

There were two big houses of learning in ancient Babylon: the House of Hillel and the House of Shamai. Hillel was an influential rabbi, who helped in the development of the Midrash and the Torah. Like Hillel, Shamai was a well-respected rabbi with his own group of followers. Both attended the same yeshivah, where they spent a great deal of their time defending their respective positions on a wide variety of biblical issues. The primary difference between them was that Shamai was disciplined and a strict adherent to Torah law, and Hillel was lenient, with a more universal perspective. Eventually, their followers felt compelled to accept the word of one or the other, and they chose Hillel because he was patient, liberal, compassionate, and understanding.

A classic story about these two rabbis has circulated for centuries. It goes something like this: One day a man approached Shamai and asked that he teach him the whole Torah while standing on one foot. Annoyed by the absurdity of the question, Shamai said, "Don't bother me. I could teach you the whole Torah standing on one foot? Are you crazy?"

So, the man went to Hillel and asked him the same question. In contrast to Shamai, Hillel balanced himself on one foot and said, "Yes, I can do that. Don't do to others what you don't want done to you. This is the Torah. The rest is all commentary."

Everyone respected Hillel's response, which revealed the essence and meaning of the Torah in less than a dozen words, and also illustrated its single and divine purpose — to "love your neighbor as yourself."

ॐ ॐ ॐ

I acquired a great deal of wisdom from my grandfather. Like the ancient rabbis, he was a non-salaried religious scholar, who paid his bills with secular full-time work. To illustrate: Moses was a herdsman when he wasn't leading his people through the desert, and Jesus was a carpenter.

With such a full agenda to juggle, it's no wonder Grandfather sometimes dropped a ball or two. At the end of one particularly busy day he neglected to turn off a chemical experiment in the lab behind his store. The entire building burned to the ground, and, because he had no insurance, he had no way to compensate for his enormous financial loss. My father, his eldest son, felt sorry for him and bought him another shop on Jaffa Road, just three blocks away from his own. Grandfather immediately equipped it with two chemical laboratories — one for himself and one for me.

Within their impeccable home, Grandfather's lovely wife, my grandmother, reigned supreme. An excellent cook, Grandmother invited the entire family to seder dinner every Passover. Grandfather always took pride in sitting at the head of the table, with my grandmother on one side of him and my father on the other. I was so close to Grandfather over the years, even across the miles, that after he passed away, the family kept his death a secret from me for an entire year. It was Uncle Isaac who volunteered to let me in on the news slowly. First, he told me that Grandfather was sick, and the story slowly progressed from there. When I began getting used to the idea that he would probably never recover, I was told the sobering truth about his passing.

The close bond I had with my grandfather reminds me of the relationship I have with my grandson, Jonathan. It's about having similar interests and compatible personalities and worldviews, as well as the combined efforts of both individuals.

My mother had four brothers, all of whom emigrated from Europe when they were young. Uncle Iz (Isaac) became a CPA in Newark, New Jersey. He was the uncle who helped me apply to the engineering school when I arrived from Israel. Uncle Eli owned a drugstore in Brooklyn, but I rarely saw him. Uncle Saul lived in Worchester, Massachusetts, and sold automobile parts. Finally, there was Uncle Leon, a tall, good-looking insurance broker with a beautiful daughter, Leah, who changed her name to Lee. Because she was my first cousin, there was no chance of romance between us, so she automatically introduced me to her girlfriend. The friend and I didn't click, but Lee and I remain good friends to this day. As I write this, she is running for city council in Great Neck Estates, New York. When Jimmy Carter was president, she was the one responsible for getting me an invitation to the White House. Eventually, she met and married a successful lawyer fourteen years her senior — and he's still alive today at 103.

๛ ๛ ๛

Summing Up

We all begin with nothing more than our DNA and our family legacy. Then we add to the mix our personality and life experience. Everyone's is unique, and yet certain of our traits and aspirations are universal and timeless. Given the tools with which we were born, each of us strives to pursue our individual dreams — what we see as our life's purpose. How we proceed to use those tools makes the difference between ultimate success and failure. And the process begins with how we were influenced, consciously or otherwise, in childhood.

Those essential life tools:

- Take notice of your interests from as far back in your youth as you can remember. They will provide insights into a natural path for your future. What you do well is often synonymous with what you enjoy doing. And what you enjoy doing makes you unique, and even sought after for your expertise.
- Refine your interests and skills.
- Be open to meeting new people and sharing a wide range of ideas.
- Develop strong relationships with others you believe to be trustworthy and with whom you share mutual support.
- Develop your intuition about people and opportunities. Learn to distinguish the genuine from the fake.
- Do not turn from risk. Without a willingness to take chances, you miss out on meeting genuine people and benefiting from great opportunities.
- Know yourself and how you want to define your life. Take appropriate action.

- Do not be deterred. Failures happen. They provide the insights for future success. The only way to avoid failure is to avoid living a full life, and that's not even an option.

❧❧❧

The best way to predict the future is to create it.

~ Abraham Lincoln

❧❧❧

CHAPTER 3

GONNA BUY A MOUNTAIN 1965

It is not the mountain we conquer but ourselves.

~ Sir Edmund Hillary

৵৵৵

New Paltz, New York, lies just across the Hudson River from Poughkeepsie. Passing through there in 1965, I was impressed by the scenic views of the river and the majesty of the surrounding mountains.

While driving leisurely around the area, I passed the Countess Mara factory, which manufactured the finest quality of men's ties and sold them to high-end haberdashers across the country. Customers who knew about their ninety percent discounts on defective merchandise took full advantage of the steep savings. Every $100 tie, even with the slightest flaw, was traditionally sold for $10 to holiday bargain hunters like my wife, Arlene. If ties have become the default men's gift over the decades, the trend may well have started at Countess Mara's annual holiday sale in New Paltz.

Situated next door to the factory was a large vacant property, which piqued my developer's curiosity. The day after I discovered the land, I dropped in to see the owner, an attorney, and learned he had obtained it from an insolvent builder as compensation for an unpaid $26,000 in legal fees. His reasoning for accepting the barter agreement was that the land, 140 acres of mountain, was slightly more valuable than the zero he would otherwise have received. Now he was willing to sell it to me for the same $26,000, which was all he had wanted in the first place — his legal fee. I haggled with him for about six months with my offer of $20,000, but finally agreed to his original asking price. Now that I owned the mountain, I was uncertain what to do with it, so I sent Yigal out to explore its potential, assuming there was any to be had. To my delight he reported back that, of the 140 acres, a full forty of them, situated around the mountain's perimeter, were flat and appropriate for development. I quickly managed to get those acres approved for lots, which I sold just as quickly for $500,000 to U.S. Homes. So, if I did nothing else with the land thereafter, I would already have made a significant profit. But the chance presented itself later on to further benefit from the mountain.

My partner and I owed $250,000 plus interest on a loan to a bank in New York City. Since we couldn't easily part with money we didn't have, we offered them the mountain, instead. To our surprise, they took it without hesitation, and without even sending one of their experts to check it out. That's how banks often work. They will take property as equity and then find the simplest way to dispose of it, which generally means a sizeable loss for them, but one they are prepared to absorb. For me, this was another important lesson learned on my path toward accumulating wealth.

The day we paid off the $250,000 loan, we stayed at the bank until late that night completing the paperwork, including signing over the 100 acres. In exchange, the bank officer returned my note. Excited about what we had accomplished, my partner and I, along with our attorney, walked over to nearby Fifth Avenue, stood in the middle of the street, lit a match to the note, and gleefully watched it burn itself out. That night we went home more than $700,000 richer.

ॐ ॐ ॐ

Summing Up

- A word to the wise investor here is to know your bank and what they are willing to take in exchange for cash. Sometimes their requirements work heavily in your favor.
- When calculating the worth of a developed property in a small town, consider the land as 10 percent of the total value and the cost of the building as 90 percent. So if the land is sold for twice as much, it only raises the value of the building by 10 percent. Even land costing 50 percent more adds only another 5 percent to the total. That's why, when buying raw land for resale, once it is developed, you could double the price and barely affect the total value of the property.
- To clarify, there is much greater upward potential for selling raw land than there is for a developed piece of property. For that reason, you can double your money on a piece of land, while never raising the price of the building on which it sits. It's a matter of supply and demand, and the need for expansion based on an ever-growing population.

Whatever happened to the hundred-acre mountain I left with the bank, I never found out — nor was I the least bit curious. I had many more mountains to climb.

ৡৡৡ

I've realized that at the top of the mountain there's another mountain.

~ Andrew Garfield

ৡৡৡ

CHAPTER 4

THE GREAT SYNAGOGUE

What we do for ourselves dies with us.
What we do for others and the world ... is immortal.

~ Albert Pine

ॐ ॐ ॐ

I moved into my unfinished offices in Manhattan's pyramid-shaped Avon building while the floors were still gray concrete. The only reason I took a suite on the forty-sixth floor of this new fifty-story building was that the four floors above me were not yet completed. Over the next few months, the contractors good-naturedly worked around and above me, and we shared a few nuggets about building construction. Then, once the fiftieth floor was completed at the top of the pyramid, its only occupant, Deutsche Bank, moved in, finally normalizing my office environment.

One day two men I had never met entered my suite without an appointment. Doctor Jaffe was a wealthy English Orthodox Jew, and his companion was the mayor of a newly incorporated city near Beersheba, in Israel's Negev Desert. They explained the details of their mission: to rebuild the Temple of Solomon, which had been destroyed by the Babylonians many centuries before. The reason the temple had not been rebuilt until now was that the Muslims had constructed their own Temple Mount over its ruins, claiming it as their Holy of Holies. Violence between the conflicting ideologies continued for years, and if the faction of extremist Jews had successfully dismantled the Muslim holy site as they threatened to do, they would likely have triggered a backlash powerful enough to ignite a world war. Instead, they wisely decided to build their synagogue in a different location — adjacent to the distinguished Palace of Solomon, the center of Judaism, where all the chief rabbis still confer on a regular basis. The Prime Minister of Israel, who, at the time, was Menachem Begin, would eventually pray there regularly in a small corner of the sanctuary with a minion of ten men.

Making a case for their grand plan, Doctor Jaffe and his colleague cited the venerable Saint Patrick's Cathedral in New York, where any Catholic dignitary could go and pray, and travelers from around the world could visit and admire. But Israel had no such equivalent. Now they would.

"The reason we're coming to you," they said, "is that you're a wealthy businessman, and you may be in a position to help us raise money for the construction."

I said, "Of course I would and I'd also contribute, personally. But I've never done anything like this before."

They smiled and said, "You'll learn."

By the time that meeting was over, I had agreed to take on the responsibility for building a great synagogue in my native Jerusalem.

The other major fundraiser on the project was England's venerable Sir Isaac Wolfson, who owned all the oil refineries in Israel. He contributed about $2 million toward the projected total cost of $40 million — half of which, $20 million, would be matched by the Israeli government. Most people who donated were Jews of faith, who envisioned their contribution as a means of preserving their heritage — not only among Israelis and other Jews, but as a shining eternal symbol of a great world religion. There were, of course, exceptions. One day soon after I began raising money, I spoke with a prosperous businessman who pledged $100,000, with one condition. He said, "I'm an atheist, so you are not to pressure me to attend services."

I said, "If you're an atheist, why do you offer your support?"

He said, "I may not believe in God, but I am a Jew and I'm committed to helping the Jewish people."

In the man's thinking, he was distinguishing between a religious belief and a covenant with his ancestral family. His perspective reminded me of the scientific definition for connecting with one's Jewishness: common memories. Most Jews agree this is the link that bonds us all as a band of brothers and sisters, and it cannot be broken. So the atheist Jew contributed his $100,000, and Sir Isaac and I raised the rest of it. Besides being a major fundraiser, I became involved with various aspects of the construction and, with the help of a local architect, I created the building's design.

One of the most striking features of the building was its magnificent stained-glass windows, and one of its most practical (because it was built for the Orthodox community) was the automated staircase I designed for use on Shabbat. The physically disabled, the elderly, and women in high heels silently applauded me for accommodating their needs.

Upon completion of construction, I was honored for my efforts and, along with Arlene, invited to pray in the sanctuary. I was also given the architect's original painting of the proposed synagogue and a huge plaque to commemorate my contributions.

Located at 60 King George Street, a beautiful wide boulevard named in honor of King George and Israel's alliance with England, the synagogue was constructed of stone in fairly simple lines and designed to blend in with the surrounding buildings. As you walk inside and to the left, you see a big plaque dedicated to Sir Isaac Wolfson, in honor of his generous donation. Although the completed structure turned out to be far less resplendent than the Temple Mount, which would have come at a prohibitive cost, it more than met my expectations.

Soon after the synagogue was open, I saw Prime Minister Begin in attendance. The image of this man in holy prayer stood in stark contrast to my youthful memory of him as the ruthless leader of a pre-1948 terrorist group. I also recall seeing him one day years later when we were both staying at the Savoy Hotel in Tel Aviv. He wore a beard and traditional clothing, looking every inch an Orthodox rabbi. If ever a man rezoned himself repeatedly, and every time successfully, it was Menachem Begin.

During this period, Arlene and I were invited to attend Sir Isaac Wolfson's eightieth birthday party in Miami, Florida. The night of the event we were presented a copy of the Bible with an inscription that read: "To Michael and Arlene Bash, co-chairs of the Great Synagogue of Jerusalem." This is the greatest memento of my lifetime, as it holds an essence of the eternal.

かかか

Summing Up

One of the most valid reasons for attaining success, along with its companion, wealth, is to be in a position to help make this world a better place — no matter how great or small a difference in the broad scheme of things. The knowledge that by your existence you have made a positive contribution to something or someone, somewhere, has the power to light your path till the end of your days, and beyond.

かかか

The meaning of life is to find your gift. The purpose of life is to give it away.

~ William Shakespeare.

かかか

CHAPTER 5

THE LUGGAGE COMPANY DEBACLE 1960s

A double-crosser is a person who borrows your pot to cook your goose in.

~ Anonymous

❧❧❧

Before this chapter, most of the stories I told you concluded with the proverbial happy ending. In that respect, I may have misled you into thinking that business success climbs a straight line to the top, and stays there forevermore. That is strongly not the case. Following is one of millions of true scenarios to illustrate that all too often bad things really do happen to good people. "Good," in this case, refers to me, your humble author. So the all-too-appropriate watchword here is: beware. If it can happen to me, it can as easily happen to you.

On the 18th floor of the Empire State Building in Manhattan was located the headquarters of a luggage company in search of a buyer, at the mindboggling bargain price of $7.25 million. I checked out the company, found it to have a sterling reputation, and wondered why the owners were willing to sell it so cheaply. After digging a little deeper, I thought I had my answer. At the time, the company's most valued client was Sears, Roebuck & Company (now commonly known as Sears), which consistently bought 60 percent of their

Featherlite luggage collection and which was now leaving New York City to establish its main headquarters in Chicago. With this change of location, it seemed logical that Sears's management would now find it cheaper to buy their luggage inventory in the Chicago area rather than pay for shipment from New York. So I called someone in the know at Sears and said, "Now that you're moving to Chicago, I'm wondering if you plan to stop ordering your luggage from the company I'm planning to buy. Too bad, too, because I was going to offer you all sorts of discounts and incentives to maintain the working relationship ...."

They said, "Not a problem. We have to ship our merchandise all across the country, anyway, and we're used to our shipping companies in New York."

That conversation convinced me I had nothing to worry about, so I decided to buy the company.

At the time, I had $1 million of the $1.25 million I needed for a down payment. One day I was meeting with the lawyers on both sides of the transaction, trying to figure a strategy for securing the additional $250,000. In the midst of our discussion, my office door swung open, and there was my devoted Arlene walking purposefully in my direction. When she reached my desk, she put her hands on her hips and asked, "Well? Have you gentlemen come up with the quarter million yet?"

I told her, "We're working on it."

"Don't agonize," she said, unclasping the showy diamond bracelet around her wrist. "This should easily get you what you need."

In that moment, my love and respect for my wife soared to the stratosphere, realizing she was willing to sacrifice her favorite bracelet to finance her husband's latest venture, however risky it might be. I shook my head and handed it back to her, but she waved it away, and promptly left the room. Once the door closed behind her, there was a discreet round of applause from the awed attorneys — all of whom envied my choice in wives.

I immediately adjourned the meeting in favor of a short trip to 47th Street, where I sold the bracelet for the requisite $250,000, deposited the funds in my account, and took my wife out to dinner at her favorite restaurant.

Now, to get the remaining $6 million. There was a well-established bank in New York, where Sidney, my rabbi-assistant, knew one of the bankers. He said to me in confidence, "If you give the man $100,000, he'll give you the $6 million loan."

Not a bad deal as bribes go, except when you realize that New York was heavily controlled by the Mafia, and that this banker was one of their guys. With some trepidation, I said, "Uh ... okay," and I gave the man the hundred thousand, in exchange for which he gave me the loan. Finally, I had the money I needed.

The only outstanding problem was that I knew nothing about the luggage business. I was buying this one only because Sidney knew the owner of a rival luggage company who was willing to work with us and build up our business. In accordance with our agreement, our new partner would get

30 percent of the profits, which seemed reasonable enough, since he would be doing all the work. Also, he had some novel ideas for creating a new line that would elevate us above our competitors and generously increase our profit margin. Things seemed to be falling nicely into place until, after sixteen years of flourishing in our working relationship, Sidney chose this particular time and place to betray me. Our standard deal in everything we had done previously constituted a seventy-thirty split in my favor. In this instance, after giving 30 percent to the other guy, Sidney finagled the percentages in such a way that between him and his friend, they would own controlling interest in the company — in essence, my junior position at 49 percent to their joint majority at 51 percent. Once I learned of Sidney's duplicity, I immediately informed him I was returning the company to its previous owner and taking the million-dollar loss. I explained that money was far less important to me than loyalty. He tried to wear me down with excuses and promises, but I had meant what I said and never wavered in the aftermath about taking the double loss — the million dollars plus the professional relationship. Over the years that followed, Sidney often tried to make amends, but that was out of the question since I could no longer trust him.

For me, trust must be earned. Once broken, it's nearly impossible to repair. I tend to abide by the overused, but highly relevant, cliché: *Fool me once, shame on you. Fool me twice, shame on me.* With millions of dollars on the line, there would be no fooling me twice.

☙☙☙

Summing Up

While you are encouraged to build and maintain your inner circle, you are wise to be selective with whomever you invite inside.

Throughout our lives we are constantly tested by the crucial question of loyalty. Make a strong effort, always, to pass that test. Otherwise, you are not only hurting others, but also yourself.

৵৵৵

No one can betray you without your permission.

~ Mahatma Gandhi

Countless others have offered the same insightful message, but in different words. That this warning comes in so many variations bares testament to its universal truth and timelessness — something on a par with the Golden Rule.

৵৵৵

CHAPTER 6

THE INCREDIBLE SWAP 1970s

A man who makes a million dollars is just as well off as if he were rich.

~ John Jacob Astor

❧❧❧

Throughout the seventies, I remained active in Dutchess County, developing land and building homes, apartment houses, and commercial centers. As you know, my specialty was rezoning — buying land zoned for single-family houses and then rezoning it to either allow for the development of multi-family units, or for commercial properties, such as retail centers or office buildings.

Around that time, the head of financing for a trade union in the Borough of Queens granted me a loan to purchase land for rezoning and construction. Coincidentally, I already owed the union $1.2 million for a mortgage on another property I had bought in the tiny town of Wappingers Falls.

One day I spotted a classified ad from a New Jersey dentist who was selling twenty acres of land in the Ulster County town of Kingston, located ninety-one miles north of New York City. The dentist, who had inherited the land from his father, was offering it for a modest $200,000. When I drove to Kingston to check it out, I discovered the land was zoned for residential use (R1) at one house per acre. My aim was to rezone it for R3, allowing me to develop the property for twenty-four apartment units per acre — four hundred eighty units in total. I immediately met with the dentist and signed a purchase agreement to buy the land at his asking price, with a 120-day escrow. In the interim, I had the land rezoned and got an appraisal for $1.2 million.

Then I spoke with the man at the union and convinced him he was better off owning a property zoned for apartment units than holding a $1.2 million mortgage on raw land in Wappingers Falls. Once we found that the union's lawyer and the dentist's lawyer were both located on Wall Street, on opposite sides of the same block, we conveniently set a closing date for the two transactions to coincide.

On the date set for closing, I followed a strictly sequenced scenario. Accompanied by my lawyer, I met with the dentist's legal counsel, paid him $200,000 in cash, and, in exchange, received a deed for the 20-acre parcel in Kingston. Then we walked across the street to meet with the union's lawyer, where I exchanged the Kingston property for the $1.2 million mortgage on the Wappingers property.

My net profit for the day: $1 million.

Some months later, I learned that the union had been involved in some unsavory dealings with the Mafia. The well-publicized investigation to follow inspired the publication of a book exposing the union's activities. One of the chapters, appropriately called "The Incredible Swap," revealed the story about my double Wall Street transaction, and how I had made

$1 million in one hour on Wall Street. Since nothing I did was illegal, I was never targeted for investigation, but, along the way, a *New York Times* writer picked up my story and wrote a feature article.

A few months later still, I received a letter from the IRS inquiring about my failure to pay taxes on the well-documented transaction. (No doubt they had read the *New York Times* article.) I sent my accountant to meet with them and give a simple, fact-based explanation on why they could not find my record of payment. As a businessman, he told them, I operated under a series of corporate entities, each of which carried a different name. They checked out my accountant's story, which they found to be correct, and that was the last I heard from the IRS.

The Boys

Whether innocently conducting business or simply going about your life in those days, you more often crossed paths with the Mafia than you realized. Of course, they didn't refer to themselves as the Mafia. They were merely "the boys." One day an Austrian woman wandered into my office for some undisclosed reason, and after she left a friend came in to warn me about her — that she was the girlfriend of one of "the boys" who was currently in jail, and that if he thought I was cutting in on his time, he would probably put out a hit on me. Fortunately, I had no interest in the man's girlfriend, but the warning reminded me of a previous encounter I had had with the Mafia.

In 1963, when I was building my first project in Upstate New York, the union built a picket line around my property and blocked a concrete truck from passing through. A representative approached me with a threatening glare and said, "This is a union job, and you have to use union labor."

I said, "Look, this is my first project. I don't have much money. What do you want me to do?"

He said, "My son is getting married, and he and his bride have their eye on a beautiful lot in one of your projects. Would you give them that lot as a wedding gift?"

I wisely said, "Absolutely. It would be my pleasure. And, by the way, congratulations!"

The picket line vanished with a wave of the union leader's hand, and I was able to get back to work. The lesson I am suggesting in light of this story is to be careful about how you conduct yourself under unfamiliar circumstances. You don't want to say no to the wrong person or — possibly worse — yes. He might be one of "the boys."

☙ ☙ ☙

Summing Up

- Read the classifieds — or whatever passes for classifieds these days. That means visiting websites like craigslist. org, eBay.com, and hundreds of others that list services, people, and products that might lead you toward a golden opportunity.

- Know what the other person wants from you, and, if so inclined, find a way to deliver it to your mutual satisfaction.
- Take pride in your business integrity. It keeps your opponents away from your door, and the IRS even further.

৵৵৵

The only person who gets paid for sticking his nose into other people's business is the tax collector.

~ Anonymous

৵৵৵

CHAPTER 7

DEEP THROAT 1972

Some types of entertainment have to be sin to be appreciated.

~ Anonymous

꙰꙰꙰

As a successful businessperson, you are often the target of people in search of investors for their pet project. Some are producers — would-be and legitimate — in need of financing for their feature film or Broadway play. This is particularly true in major U.S. cities, such as Los Angeles and New York, where arts and entertainment are a major industry.

I had an office on 53rd Street and Seventh Avenue, head-quarters for my real estate business. Next door to me was the office of Louis "Butchie" Peraino, who owned Plymouth Distributing, which he later renamed Arrow Film and Video. One day, Peraino walked into my office and introduced himself. "Do you know anything about blue movies?"

I said, "No. Not a thing."

"Well, I'm going to produce one in black-and-white. Nothing like this has ever been done before — a porn film with a real plot. It'll take six days to shoot on a budget of $25,000. Invest with me and I guarantee you'll make at least $100,000. I've got a girl from California flying in today to interview for the lead and, if I like what I see, I'll sign her on for $1,000."

"Sounds like a good deal."

"Well, if you're in, I'll need a check for $10,000."

Caught up in the fervor, and before even glancing at the screenplay, I wrote Lou a check for $10,000. Within the hour, a modestly attired Linda Lovelace (her last name newly minted by Lou) walked through the front door. Linda's face was not the first thing about her to catch Peraino's attention but, in his dubious defense, he did not ask her to lift her skirt or unbutton her blouse. All he did was wander over to her, place a hand over each of her breasts, and apply a little pressure. A satisfied grin crossed his lips, and he hired her on the spot.

Later that day, I took the screenplay home to read, and left it on top of a prominent table. Arlene noticed it, picked it up, and read it all the way through. The experience did not make her happy. "Michael," she said. "You're not thinking of getting involved with this smutty movie, are you?" I said nothing. She continued. "I'm surprised at you. You're the father of four children and a respectable businessman. Don't you know how it would look for you to be associated with something like this? Promise me you'll tell the guy you can't be involved … and just get your money back."

After listening to Arlene so vehemently express her opinion, I picked up the script and read it through as objectively as I could. Without checking my reflection in the mirror, I was sure my face was a bright shade of scarlet. Arlene had won her case.

The next morning, I walked into Peraino's office and told him I was out. "My wife read the screenplay and is adamantly against my participation. So I read it, myself, and I have to agree with her. It would upset our young children and put me in a bad light with my colleagues. I'm sure you understand. Just give me back my check, and we'll put this behind us."

Peraino stared at me, unsmiling. "I can't do it, Bash. You gave me your word, and now you're backing out. That's not how it works. You're an entrepreneur ... you should know better."

He was right. My naïveté had just cost me $10,000.

Soon thereafter Lou took the script to the Mafia and got what he needed, which was $22,500 for the entire production. His father, Anthony Peraino, a member in good standing of the Colombo crime family, covered the additional $25,000 for the cost of music. In order to separate his professional image from his father's "line of work," Lou adopted the neutral name of Lou Perry for his film credit and he gave his writer/director, Gerard Damiano, the rights to one-third of the revenues. But once the film became a money machine Lou forced Damiano out of the partnership and paid him off with the paltry sum of $25,000. And that's what happens when you trust someone inherently untrustworthy.

Those were the days when the much beloved Johnny Carson emceed NBC's *Tonight Show*, and his influence impacted all levels of society. One night soon after the film's release, when Johnny told his audience that he had seen this highly provocative porn film and enjoyed it, he ignited a firestorm that took years to extinguish. Inadvertently Carson's endorsement made millions in profit for Lou's father and his crime family.

The added controversy of an obscenity trial only added to the film's perverse allure. Overnight it became the go-to film in the newly created category of "porn chic," and so it remained for decades to come.

Consequently, in its first seven weeks of release, *Deep Throat* grossed $1 million and, in its opening week at New York City's New World Theater, it broke a porn film single-screen record of $30,033. Six months later, the gross receipts were tallied at $3 million. Within forty-eight weeks of its release, *Variety* ranked it among the top ten highest-grossing films. When compared with box office figures of today, these grosses seem meager, but considering that in 1972 first-run movie tickets were selling for $5 each, the perception swiftly changes.

Over the years, the film continued to control conversations, public and private. Even politics co-opted its legacy when Washington journalist Bob Woodward used the provocative title as code name for W. Mark Felt, the heretofore secret informer in the Nixon-Watergate scandal.

To put this phenomenon into perspective, whereas most studio-produced features played theaters for no more than a week in the 1970s, the Pussycat Theater in Los Angeles ran this low-budget independent film for ten years straight. Johnny Carson aside, how did a porn film gain such national attention? Probably because it came at a time when it was the first of its kind — an X-rated feature-length film with enough production value and word-of-mouth that it was virtually destined to become a cult classic. More than forty-five years after its release, *Deep Throat* remains the highest grossing pornographic feature film in history.

How high those grosses go remains the subject of controversy. Some estimates are as high as $300 million to $600 million — an almost impossible number — while others settle into a more realistic range. Whatever the accurate figure, if I had remained in the partnership, it would still have reaped me far greater profit than all my years as a real estate developer — and that has been considerable. Of course, this scenario assumes that Lou Peraino would not have cut me off at $25,000, as he did his writer/director. If he had, considering the lesson I had already learned from my failed relationship with Sidney, I would only have had myself to blame.

๑๑๑

Summing Up

Great opportunities present themselves to most of us from time to time, promises of sky-high returns in exchange for little to no money or effort up front. Yet, for one reason or another, the part of us that accounts for our character, integrity, and moral values forbids us from becoming involved. In the aftermath, despite those massive profits we let pass us by, we have no sound reason for regret.

The lesson I learned from *Deep Throat* was far more valuable than anything I could have earned from its box office receipts. Shakespeare's Polonius spoke to it in *Hamlet*, Act I,

Scene 3: "This above all: to thine own self be true, And it must follow, as the night the day, Thou canst not then be false to any man."

ॐॐॐ

A building has integrity, just like a man. And just as seldom.

~ Ayn Rand

ॐॐॐ

CHAPTER 8

BROADWAY TO ST. JUDE LATE 1970s

Broadway is a main artery of New York — a hardened artery.

~ Walter Winchell

❧❧❧

Toward the end of the decade, my family and I moved downstate to New City, about twenty minutes' drive to Manhattan — close enough for a convenient commute and just far enough that my children could enjoy the benefits of upscale small-town living. Five days a week I would drive across the George Washington Bridge and park at 9 West 57th Street, where, from 1976 to 1979, I leased office space.

My First Bought-and-Paid-For Family Home

The house we had bought in New City for $80,000 was the most expensive in the area. And as relatively inexpensive as it was, even at the time, it was the first house for which I paid with actual currency. As you have already learned, the much larger house on Yates Boulevard in Poughkeepsie was built about ten years before and cost me zero in terms of real dollars because every one of the contractors I was using on the construction of a 360-unit apartment building agreed to perform the same task for my new family home. That included plumbing, electrical, framing, interior design, and every other essential plus a few luxuries, besides. When the house was finally finished, it had a market value of $60,000. The two lots on which I built were my only costs, a total of $10,000, or $5,000 each. A few years later, when I finally sold the property, it was worth $120,000. My buyer didn't have the entire amount in cash, so he gave me two lots he had recently purchased as his initial payment of $10,000. I gave them to Charlie Patrick, who subsequently sold them for $24,000 — $12,000 apiece. So I made money on that transaction, as well. I was learning that the more experienced you are, the better prepared you are to tap into the opportunities around you. And if they don't exist, you simply create them.

You may recall that the only drawback to this freebie formula was that it took considerably more time to build the house than it would have otherwise, since its completion depended on the concurrent completion of those apartment units I was building. Rather than the three months a house like that might have otherwise taken to construct, it took a full year. But since I was just starting out, I found the financial advantages I gained far outweighed the frustrating element of time.

In the interim, I bought some lots in Beechwood Park, a couple of blocks away. Included in the sale was a house in which our growing family took up residence until our new home was finished.

Anyone planning to develop a large multi-unit property while also building a private home might use the same strategy as I did and save enormous sums of money.

The Business That There's No Business Like

As much as writers, producers, and performers court investors for their ability to make their dreams come true, the investors are just as likely — and maybe more so — to be drawn into those dreams. At least, that's how I explain my investment in six separate on- and off-Broadway plays during the decade of the seventies, most of them forgettable flops. But being this close to Manhattan, I was enjoying the best of both worlds — the cultural and glamour of the big city and the profitability of suburban real estate. I may have passed on the classic porn film, but these projects, mediocre as they turned out to be, carried an air of respectability and Arlene's gold seal of approval.

Although I never made a profit investing in any of those shows, I never lost, either. And that is because I took the conservative route by investing in backers' auditions. Before a play is produced, it is nothing more than a script and a producer whose task it is to "shop it around" for funding. Once a few potential investors are corralled, a reading is scheduled to persuade as many as possible to commit a large sum of money to the cause. And so, for about $100,000 each, I enjoyed the excitement of helping to produce a few Broadway plays. I did this with little to no risk, since I was always among the first to get back my initial investment.

Two of the plays I produced are credited as follows:

Wheelbarrow Closers: Broadway production of original play by Raymond Serra

Producers: Tony Conforti, in association with Howard Effron and George Tunick
Associate Producers: Michael Bash, Howard Wesson, Irving Warshaftig

The show played for eight performances at the Bijou Theater, from October 11, 1979, to October 16, 1979. With all the talent, time, and money that went into a failed production like this, the public's ultimate disinterest was toughest on the actors and stage crew, whose hopes for a long-running paycheck were quickly dashed.

> *It's one of the tragic ironies of the theatre that only one man in it can count on steady work — the night watchman.*
>
> ~ Tallulah Bankhead

Manny: Broadway production of original play by Raymond Serra
Producers: Robert R. Blume, Tony Conforti, Manny Taustine
Associate Producers: Michael Bash, Howard Effron

Set in Washington, D.C., and Beverly Hills from 1927 to 1973, *Manny* played 31 performances at the Century Theater from April 18, 1979, to May 13, 1979. This one lasted less than a month, which was a surprise, considering that it was based on the life story of the legendary Hollywood and stage star, Edward G. Robinson.

Perhaps my greatest discovery of talent during that period was actor Danny Aiello, who was a New York cabdriver when I met him, doing his best to support his wife and kids. Within a short period of time following our meeting, he was acting on the Broadway stage in *Wheelbarrow Closers*, directed by actor Paul Sorvino. Although the play flopped, Danny went on to appear in other productions, none of which was noteworthy, except by their short-lived runs. Rather than give up on his dreams of a lasting career, Danny wisely "rezoned" himself for Hollywood, where he has since enjoyed a long and lucrative run in motion pictures, including his stint in *The Godfather II* and his classic role as Cher's clueless boyfriend in the Oscar-nominated *Moonstruck*.

Make Room for Charity

Through Danny and another Broadway actor I barely knew, I was introduced to Danny Thomas, the beloved and legendary film and TV star. Although he has long since passed away, Danny and his legacy live on through St. Jude's Children's Research Hospital, which he founded in 1962, and which his children, Marlo, Terre, and Tony, continue to oversee. Upon meeting him, I agreed to help Danny raise money for his telethon, which was held in New York City every May on Channel 9. Without exception, we amassed ten to twenty million dollars annually for the hospital — thanks in great part to guest appearances by some of Danny's famous friends, like Dean Martin, Frank Sinatra, and Joey Bishop. On one occasion, Bob Hope invited my twelve-year-old daughter to come onstage and join him in a duet of "Thanks for the Memory." One year, Danny asked my father to participate in the show. Fluent as he was in Arabic, and knowing that Danny was Lebanese and also spoke Arabic, Father engaged him in bilingual conversation throughout the entire telecast.

At every telethon without exception, I would sit in the front row. Each time Danny came down the aisle, headed toward the stage, he would stop at my seat, talk with me, hug me, and kiss me. When we had dinner together, he would fuss over my children. He even had a nickname for my wife — "Rocks" — inspired by that blinding twenty-carat diamond I had placed on her third finger, left hand.

I was friendly with Joey Bishop through a man named Stan Loehman. Stan's brother, Lee, was an agent with William Morris and booked talent for clubs, which meant that there was scarcely a restaurant table in town he couldn't book for himself, last minute. Through Lee, I, too, was able to reserve a table at the most popular night spots in New York, including the Copacabana, where I dined with stars like Don Rickles and Ed Sullivan. I was also friendly with Hy Einhorn, who booked acts for the Catskill Mountains, and with whom I went into business. It was through Einhorn that I met the legendary comedian, Henny Youngman. Hy eventually became famous for turning down Barbra Streisand for agency representation, based, superficially, on the size of her nose, which she wisely chose never to shorten. Talk about missed opportunities — Hy's, not Barbra's!

৵৵৵

Summing Up

I repeat this because it's so crucial: One major advantage of success is having the opportunity to reach out and help others. Indirectly, you are also helping yourself.

From that land of missed opportunities, be aware that some of the best of them arrive in plain brown paper. Take the time to unwrap and examine them before passing them over. And even then, think hard before making your final decision. Mostly they are not scandalous film projects financed by unsavory sources. But neither are they likely to make you rich. And sometimes that's okay. There can be far more to an opportunity than a dollar sign.

ఈఈఈ

Any good that I can do or any kindness that I can show to any human being, let me do it now. Let me not defer or neglect it, for I shall not pass this way again.

~ Mahatma Gandhi

ఈఈఈ

CHAPTER 9

CONVERTING A FAILING BUSINESS INTO A THRIVING PROFIT CENTER 1978–1981

A wise man will make more opportunities than he finds.

~ Francis Bacon

ॐ ॐ ॐ

One day in late 1978 I was riding an elevator in the Empire State Building with two gentlemen, one of whom I recognized as media giant Rupert Murdoch. Having nothing better to do but stare at the door, I eavesdropped as he told the other man, whom I assumed was his attorney, "On those four magazines we're publishing ... I've already spent $12 million, and I'm losing more by the minute. Let's unload them."

With little time left to give my "elevator speech" or even to prepare it, I instinctively interrupted, told Murdoch I was an entrepreneur, and that I would love to buy his publishing business. My reasoning was, "You're going to close them down, anyway ...."

"Okay," he said, instinctively. "Give me a hundred thousand, and it's all yours."

We approached his designated floor, and I accompanied him and his attorney out of the elevator. He quickly informed me he had a controlled circulation of 500,000 on the four publications, which he distributed free of charge to recent college graduates. There was the *New Engineer* for engineers and *MBAs* for MBAs and *Medical Horizons* for medical school graduates and *Juris Doctor* for law school graduates. Without hesitation, I followed him to his lawyer's office to close the deal. Coincidentally, I even had a blank check with me. My on-the-spot thinking was that here was a titan of business, who spent $12 million on something he believed held value. It had to be worth at least the hundred thousand he quoted me. Rather than waste time and momentum checking out his records, I signed the check over to him before either of us could change our minds.

My New Free Business, Plus Perks

The office for my new enterprise was located on the seventh floor of 770 Lexington Avenue, where, upon arrival the next morning, I met with my team of thirty editors. Casually, I asked the editor-in-chief, "How much do we have in our bank account?"

He said, "A hundred and fifty thousand."

Swallowing my surprise, I said, "Write me a check for a hundred thousand."

So, overnight, I had essentially acquired a publishing business without investing a cent of my own money. I couldn't help but wonder why Murdoch hadn't, at least, taken out the available cash before selling to a stranger. The only answer I could come up with was that he had no idea it existed. I'm second-guessing here, but probably the editor would call him periodically and ask him to issue another check for business expenses — and then another — until far more was going into the kitty than was coming out. Considering the number of Murdoch's business enterprises, it was understandable this one had been getting less of his attention than the others, a condition for which I was exceedingly grateful.

But there was more. The editor wasn't finished confiding in me about company assets. Now he told me there was a DX card. A lot of the company's advertising was done on a barter basis, and we had $400,000 in credit with jewelry stores, high-end restaurants, hotels in Florida and California — all sorts of freebies. I was naturally taken aback by this delightfully unexpected news, so I asked, "Didn't he ever use the card?"

He said, "He didn't know we had it."

Not only had my new business not cost me a cent, it had even dropped $400,000 of credit into my lap. Using it up was not easy, since over time we kept accumulating more — and still more. It took four years of strict dedication to use it all.

Another benefit I realized was that the office was furnished at least as beautifully as my own on 57th Street, where I still paid a high rent. So with no need for two luxury offices, I transferred my real estate operation over to Lexington Avenue, except for my expensive furnishings, which I sold for an excellent price. The consolidation saved me a lot of money.

Then, just as I was beginning to think I had run out of perks, I found I was able to borrow $350,000 from a Swedish bank in New York, based solely on the publishing company's assets.

After trying to make sense of my unearned windfall, I took time to learn about the company's operations and how to design strategies for improving its income. Most of the paid advertising was comprised of image ads from major companies like IBM and General Motors, attempting to influence the purchasing power of young professionals. Each of the advertisers bought six ads a year at a monthly cost of $25,000 — or an annual total of $150,000. The four magazines were always published simultaneously. Most of the content was identical, except for a few pages related to subject matter specific to each of the professions — and, of course, there were the different titles and covers. Using his failed strategy, Murdoch had been losing $500,000 a year. I couldn't afford to lose five dollars. Since the client companies advertised only six months out of the year, I considered closing shop for the alternate six months that advertising space went unsold, but the idea struck me as uncharacteristically shabby. On the other hand, nine months of publishing and three months off for summer vacation — that seemed wholly reasonable. With the monthly cost of printing the magazines at $250,000, in just those three months without publication I would save $750,000. That meant not only would I not be losing $500,000, I would actually be profiting $250,000. Why hadn't this simple equation occurred to Murdoch and his management team?

Now it was down to business. The magazines were printed in another state. I called the printer and bargained with him for a reduced rate — but without success. Then I sent in my son David to negotiate, and he managed to forge a better deal.

Next, in order to confirm my readership of 500,000, I called in the ABC Company, whose business it was to verify numbers. If my records proved correct, I would be eligible for ads from those companies that traditionally demanded a verification search. It surprised me that some major corporations merely accepted the numbers we supplied them, whereas liquor distillers did not. While I knew our figures were accurate, how did *they* know? Each month we simply sent them a tear sheet and an invoice, in response to which they automatically remitted a check. No questions. No complaints. No regrets.

It was becoming commonplace for me by now to associate with famous people, in some cases even before fame touched their lives. Through the publishing company, I eventually developed a working relationship with celebrated runner James Fixx, who wrote the bestselling book on running, and eventually died of a heart attack while jogging. Fixx worked for me during his pre-celebrity days, but once his huge publishing profits started pouring in, he no longer needed the job. P.S. He resigned, owing me $3,000.

By the early 1980s, the market had turned, and companies were cutting back on their advertising, particularly their image ads. When I did the math and saw the magazines were no longer making a profit, I wasted no time closing down the operation and liquidating everything: the thirty desks, thirty pay phones, thirty typewriters — every last stick of furniture and equipment. The one thing I kept was a trial phone for which the phone company had never sent a bill. Benefactor of AT&T's billing mistake was my family in Israel, who heard from me a lot more frequently for a while, and it wasn't costing any of us a dime.

Know When to Call it a Day

Because I had been lucky enough to meet Rupert Murdoch that day on the elevator, I enjoyed an excellent and profitable run in the publishing business. On the other hand, luck was only one of the requisite elements. Another was precision timing. Think about it: if either Murdoch or I had missed that elevator by a couple of seconds, we would never have met. But the third and most important element was that few people would have seized on such a tiny window of opportunity. I had to be curious, confident, and capable of making a smart and split-second decision, and then to act upon it. Of course, I then had to have the imagination to make a go of the business, however relatively short-term it turned out to be.

A couple of years ago, I called the legendary Murdoch and reminded him that I had bought his magazine business years before. He had no time for chatter. "Yes. What do you want?"

I told him I had written and published a book, and wondered if he would be willing to give me a review or to advertise it for me in his newspaper. He said that all he had was the *Wall Street Journal*, and that it didn't publish book reviews. The bottom line was that he was cordial and he had taken my call. Never mind that this was only after my secretary had called him repeatedly, without success. The point I make here is that there is something to be said for dogged persistence.

This entire chapter in my life lasted from 1978 to 1981 or so, and can be counted as an overall success. But if I hadn't quit when I did, I would have started bleeding money like Murdoch had done, and without the resources to buffer me between billions.

ત*ત*ત*

Summing Up

Don't discount the forces of nature in your pursuit of success. Certainly, the issue of timing worked impeccably in my favor throughout this endeavor — as it has to a greater or lesser extent in most of my enterprises. But timing is nothing without follow-through.

Conversely, I advise restraint in committing to too many projects at once. Regardless of your good intentions, you cannot do them all with equal efficiency. Besides, you always want to leave space in your life for that next opportunity.

ત*ત*ત*

There is no scarcity of opportunity to make a living at what you love.
There is only a scarcity of resolve to make it happen.

~ Wayne Dyer

ત*ત*ત*

CHAPTER 10

CASTLE TO MONEY PIT TO CONVENTION CENTER AND BACK AGAIN 1979–1982

One man's home is another man's business opportunity.

~ The author

ৰ্চৰ্চৰ্চ

A man named Rosenfeld worked for a small English bank in New York. In 1979, thanks to a local business connection, he was able to buy homes at a good price, which he would upgrade and sell. One day he approached me about a castle he was purchasing in Great Barrington, a town in Western Massachusetts on the New York border. According to Mr. Rosenfeld, the asking price was a measly $1.5 million, whereas the building costs had exceeded $100 million. He had planned to promote the estate as a tourist attraction, but given its remote location, he realized too late that its chance for generating profit was all but nil.

The story behind the castle is that in 1881 Mary Hopkins of San Francisco, wealthy widow of Mark Hopkins (part-owner of Southern Pacific Railroad), commissioned interior designer Edward Searles to redecorate her mansion on Nob Hill — present-day site of the landmark Mark Hopkins Hotel. She was so delighted with the results of his efforts that she rehired him, this time to build her a castle in her hometown of Great Barrington. With no budgetary constraints on his work, Searles imported the finest artifacts and marbles from Europe, and employed the best masons and woodworkers. In 1887, the growing collaboration between Hopkins and Searles culminated in marriage, which is naturally how the mansion came to be known as Searles Castle.

The property consisted of about forty-five rooms, a huge swimming pool, a nine-hole golf course, and a restaurant. It also had a concert hall with a sixty-five-foot ceiling, and accommodated about five hundred people. After wondering what I could do with something that displayed all the earmarks of failure, I decided to rezone it into something practical, like a convention center. But that would require a convenient place for visitors to stay overnight. Fortunately, the small motel across the street was also available for purchase. So I bought both properties and effectively started yet another chapter in my evolving professional life.

In order for the bank to lend me the $1.5 million I needed, they demanded a cash deposit of $400,000, which I didn't have. At the time, bank CDs were yielding an inflated 16 percent. So, a 5-year CD with a value of $1 million could be had for as little as $400,000. I went to the Bank Leumi, which issued me the $1 million in CDs for the requisite $400,000. Then I took the CDs to the Bank of New York, where I got a loan of $1 million against the $1 million in CDs. The Bank of New York sent a messenger to Bank Leumi with the $1 million, and, in exchange for the check, they gave him the CDs. The bank took their $400,000, and I was left with $600,000, which I used for down payments on the castle and the motel. (At times like these, an entrepreneur is grateful for having passed high school math.)

As a means of promoting the castle, I hired an Oxford-English-speaking narrator to host a series of TV commercials highlighting the British theme. Then, on Halloween night, I threw a gala costume party, at which all the fictional monsters ever imagined were in attendance and scaring the daylights out of one another.

An added benefit of the location was its proximity to Lenox and its annual Tanglewood Music Festival. But because of the area's remoteness, there was little else of interest to the general public. And that was the fatal flaw in this otherwise fairytale adventure of mine.

Some visitors came to tour the castle for the $10 price of admission, but the conventions and conferences I had envisioned never came to fruition. In 1981, after two years of mediocre profits, I decided to sell. Rosenfeld had warned me of the drawbacks. I just didn't pay attention. Although the castle was making money, it wasn't enough to justify my time and investment. In the following year, an insurance company paid me $2 million for the property, which they would use for their archives and corporate retreats. As for the motel, I sold it back to the original owners at the same price I paid for it. When I walked away it was with $500,000 in profit and memories of being king of a castle.

At the same time I was living in the New England castle, my brother was involved with a fast-food chain in South Carolina — which you will read about in the next chapter. Many of my projects overlapped. This was just one of them.

ఛ ఛ ఛ

Summing Up

Lesson learned from the castle investment was similar to what I took away from the Murdoch enterprise. To borrow from Kenny Rogers — *you have to know when to hold 'em* ... and, you know the rest. I enjoyed this professional interlude, but more for fun than profit. At such times in your life that you can afford the luxury, a dip into diversion requires no defense. But even then, there's a limit.

ఛ ఛ ఛ

Sometimes a castle is nothing more than a white elephant with a large expense account.

~ The author

ఛ ఛ ఛ

CHAPTER 11

FAST TALK AND FAST FOOD 1981–1982

Something fishy this way comes.

> ~ inspired by Ray Bradbury's
> *Something Wicked This Way Comes*

కొకొకొ

One morning in 1981, when Yigal was reading the *Wall Street Journal*, he saw an ad from a businessman named Bond (not his real name), who owned a chain of 245 fast-food restaurants called Cedric's Fish & Chips. Bond was in Chapter 11 and was forced to sell. Yigal loved the idea of running a fast-food chain, and said to me, "Let's buy these restaurants, and I'll run the operation for you." The company's central office was in Columbia, South Carolina, which made it geographically inconvenient for us in the Northeast, although Yigal didn't consider it a problem. He said, "Every Monday morning I'll just fly to Columbia and fly back Friday night to spend the weekend with family."

So, we flew to Columbia and met with Bond, who wanted $2 million for the business. Naturally I asked him why he went bankrupt. He readily admitted to having wasted his money on expensive cars and other luxury items he couldn't afford. That made sense to us. Mr. Bond wasn't the first businessman we met who had spent more than he earned, and then was left with no option but to sell his enterprise. While it's a sad situation for the owner, it often presents a golden opportunity for outside investors. Yigal and I expressed our interest in making a deal, but there was the outstanding matter of being $2 million short, and the question of where to get it.

Through my attorney I met Greg Lauter (another fictitious name). On our first meeting Greg insisted on giving me an unsolicited $100,000. He said he saw that I needed the money. I didn't question his reasoning. I asked him how soon he wanted me to pay him back. He said, "Whenever you have it. No problem." I remind you this was $100,000 in late 1970s dollars, which is equal to about $400,000 in today's currency. Not a sum most people would lend on a first meeting — and certainly not without, at least, settling on a strict schedule for reimbursement.

Lauter, who was an American of Polish and German descent, lived in New Jersey's Wall Township and sold property insurance for ship cargo, a business that had made him a multimillionaire. What distinguished Greg from his insurance competitors was that he never bothered to purchase the policies he was paid to secure for his clients. His excuse was, *No one ever submits a claim, anyway, so why spend the money?* And he was right — under most circumstances. Then an anomaly happened with one of his clients, who filed a legitimate claim against his insurer. When the policyholder found out there was no policy, Greg was in deep trouble. So deep, in fact, he was willing to pay his own lawyer a million dollars just to get him out of the mess. The lawyer gladly obliged. So when in our first meeting I told him I needed $2 million, and explained what I needed it for, he said, "I'm in." Just like that. Not only did he see this as a good opportunity for Yigal, but for his adopted Jewish son, whom he envisioned sharing in the operation.

While Greg didn't have the needed capital, he did have an AAA-rated General Obligation Bond from Texas. To make it easier to follow this story, I provide this brief tutorial on bond interest: Generally, interest runs 5 to 7 percent. Texas offers two kinds of these bonds. One gives a normal 5 percent (0.05) return, which means that if you invest $1,000 you get $50 annual interest. A second, cheaper, bond offers .005, which provides an annual yield of $5 on the $1,000 investment — or 10 percent of 5 percent, which returns 10 percent of what you would otherwise get with the standard 5 percent return. A 30-year bond would return your investment, plus 5 percent a year, equaling $2,500 or 150 percent. (If you're still with me, we can now return to the story.)

When I took the bond to Barclay's Bank, I told the banker, "I need $2 million. How much stock do I have to give you?" He said he would have to talk to the people at the bond fund to determine its current value, and, when he did, they quoted him the value of the .05 bond, instead of the .005. "No. It's actually .005," I told him.

The banker was clearly annoyed with me, and said, "Hey, don't teach me the banking business. Just stick to your real estate."

I said, "Okay. You don't want me to teach you … I won't teach you." So, I gave him $3 million worth of bonds to get back $2.4 million in cash.

Due to the banker's stubbornness, he had given me 80 percent return at 0.5 percent rather than what I was actually due at .005.

Delighted with the outcome of the banking mistake, Greg gave me enough stock, which cost him much less than he had anticipated, to secure the financing. So, primarily due to a banker's shortsightedness and my own alertness and sense of honesty, I was abundantly rewarded.

Now that we had 245 restaurants in about a dozen Southern states, including the Carolinas and Virginia, we had to do another type of rezoning. Yigal visited all of those locations and told me about everything he had learned along the way — including whatever there was to know about Hush Puppies, besides their ability to appease hunger. As a result of his vigilance, he discovered that, out of all the branches we owned, forty-five of them were losing money. He told me not to ask any questions, not to even try to improve them, simply to shut them down. Now we were left with 200 of the original 245. As soon as we closed the bad ones, we began to make a profit. In the meantime, Yigal compensated us for the closed locations by opening new ones in New York and New Jersey. My brother was doing an excellent job with the company, and I was proud of him.

Concerned about making his twenty-something son happy, Greg had built him a big house in the middle of Wall Township, with a courtyard and pool. But the son constituted a growing problem. He was difficult to get along with and fought with Yigal on a nightly basis. I would often spend three hours making peace between them, only to see the fighting resume on the following evening. With no peace treaty in sight, I realized there was only one solution. I told Greg, "Look, I see no way to stop this fighting. Either you buy me out or I buy you out."

Greg said, "I'll buy you out. Otherwise what would I do with my son? He loves the business."

Internal fighting is a primary cause for co-owners to bail out of a viable business. Ours was a classic case.

My priorities were now elsewhere, anyway. Arlene and I would soon be moving to California and I had no interest in seeing Greg again. When the loan came due on the restaurants, however, he refused to pay. The bank manager who had granted the loan at Barclay's Bank sent me a letter that said, "You were right. You told us the value of the bonds was lower, and we ignored you. As a result, we are not holding you responsible for any portion of the loan."

I was most impressed with the British bank's equitable policy. Had it been an American financial institution, I might not have fared as well. Unfortunately, as is often the case with people of integrity, the banker, whose decision it had been to grant the loan, got the worst of the deal. He was summarily transferred to a remote branch somewhere in South Africa.

A year or two later, when my family and I were already living in California, a front-page story broke in the *Wall Street Journal* about an insurance agent who had failed to insure his clients with policies they had purchased from him. Greg was sentenced to ten years in prison for his intentional oversight, but after a successful shot at plea-bargaining he got his sentence reduced to five. What Greg left behind was a directory that listed his four hundred business contacts — worth millions to an entrepreneur looking for ad revenue, but nothing at all to a convicted felon cooling his heels behind bars. Over the years, I never again heard from or about Greg or his combative adopted son. I considered myself lucky.

❧❧❧

Summing Up

The Talmud says: "The end for a thief is the gallows." If you steal repeatedly over the years, eventually you get caught and likely for something far more insidious than theft. That's the moral lesson of this particular tale — and, in today's climate of greed and corruption, it's priceless.

❧❧❧

Men are not hanged for stealing horses,
but that horses may not be stolen.

~ Halifax

Or, to look at it from a more perverse perspective …

Men are not arrested for stealing …
They are arrested for being caught at it.

~ Anonymous

❧❧❧

CHAPTER 12

BEEF CATTLE AND DAIRY COWS: MILKING THE MILK MARKET 1983–1991

If you ask me, 'So what is your business model?'
Our business model's always about shifting to higher
value opportunities.

~ Ginni Rometty,
Chairperson/President/CEO, IBM

჻჻჻

In 1982, I rezoned my family geographically from New York City to Newport Beach, California. This was not a business decision, but based on several factors, mostly personal. For one thing, Arlene wanted to be near her sister, who lived in Tustin, not far from our new home. For another, having grown up in Israel, I never liked the extremes of New York weather — freezing in winter and muggy and hot in summer. Even Arlene, a native New Yorker, had had her fill of it. But as anxious as was our youngest, Jeremy, to become a Californian, his new classmates at the Costa Mesa high school he attended made his transition difficult. They teased him mercilessly about his clothing, habitually accusing him of wearing the "wrong kind" of jeans or shirt. Jeremy was discovering the hard way that Southern California kids had their own unique look, and that

anything that varied from the norm was unacceptable, including the wearer. Before long, Jeremy had rezoned himself into a
"California dude" and, from then on, he was considered cool
enough to fit in. Sometimes you *do* have to do as the Romans
do, just to get by — as long as it doesn't mean giving up who
you are.

Our first residence in Newport Beach was an apartment
on 17th Street, where we lived for a year. Then we bought a
6,500-square-foot house in Big Canyon that included a garage
apartment, where I hung my original paintings and where Joel
set up his private bedroom. Arlene quickly adjusted to Newport and became involved in charity work, as she had done
in New York. She even helped build an old age facility for
the Jewish community. With her nursing background, helping
people was the natural next step for her.

Once the family began acclimating, I followed suit. That
meant concentrating on ways to duplicate my earlier successes
on the East Coast. Since it requires money to make money,
I immediately forged a relationship with the Beverly Hills
branch of Israel's Bank Hapoalim.

Next I contacted some real estate developers whose ads I
had seen in the *Wall Street Journal*. I met with them on Katella
Road in Anaheim and impressed them with my background.
When I mentioned I could probably get them funding for one
of their pet projects, they suggested we join forces. To seal the
deal, they treated me to a $1,000 champagne dinner at a chic
Costa Mesa restaurant. In addition, they gave me a sporty yellow Mercedes to drive and an attractive office in their facilities,

where I quickly made friends with the owner and his second-in-command. After subsequent lunches and dinners with these men, it occurred to me what they were doing, and it wasn't buying land, as they led their investors to believe. They were merely fulfilling their promise to them, which was 22 percent return on investment. To be more specific, their investors were getting back nothing more than interest on their own money — a classic ploy named for legendary schemer Charles Ponzi, and later perfected, to a point, by convicted felon Bernie Madoff. This scam being perpetrated by my new partners was the first Ponzi scheme I had seen close up, and I wanted no part of it. Thus I walked away from my first business deal in Southern California, and said goodbye to my lovely new office on Katella Road and my cool yellow Mercedes.

Since the real estate market was in a downturn in the early eighties, the timing was right for me to focus on a new business model and, once again, rezone my career path. Then I met a likeable New Zealander named Harry Holt, who did time-sharing on boats and condos, and ran a legitimate business on the side. Harry had a ranch in Temecula, California, near Lake Elsinore, where he applied the technique of embryo transfer to improve the quality of beef cows. Not knowing a thing about cattle, I was lucky to have Harry teach me everything he knew on the subject. Based on notes he had collected from several clients, I was able to get him a loan of a few million dollars. Then we began selling his investments, which turned out to be a short-lived enterprise, as I was used to working on my own. Announcing my departure, I told Harry I planned to build a business similar to his, but would not compete with him in California.

Through a 1983 magazine article I learned about the Longcriers, a father and son who were doing things similar to Holt, but at their ranch in Mineola, eighty miles east of Dallas, Texas. I called and invited them to talk with me in Newport Beach, and our visit was so successful that I made a deal with them to invest in cattle. In order to raise the necessary funds, I hired a talented businessman named Lee Luxon, who began sending out letters of solicitation to qualified investors. Along the way, Lee opened a total of seven offices for us, including one in New York City, which became his headquarters. Tax shelters were providing strong incentives among certain industries at the time, and this type of cattle ranching was one of them.

As with Harry Holt, the Longcriers' business model was to perform embryo transfers on cattle to breed the best beef cows in the country. We cross-bred the premium quality Simmentals with Brahmans — a tough breed used to living in extremely arid conditions. After trying various ratios, including fifty-fifty, we settled on what seemed the best of our estimates: five-eighths Simmental and three-eighths Brahman, the combination of which produced a hybrid we called Simbra.

Because of their experience in the field, the Longcriers controlled most of the business and would regularly fly to their ranch to oversee the breeding process. My contribution was to bring in investors, in exchange for which I received a portion of their larger business.

At the New York office one day in 1985, an Israeli named Meir Braun informed Lee Luxon that the same method the Texas Longcriers used for breeding superior beef cows was a variation of what his employer was doing with milk cows in Upstate New York. But, rather than provide a greater quality of meat for the general public, these cows were bred to yield a greater quantity of milk. I was intrigued by the concept of embryo transfer and asked Meir's employer to come meet with me in Newport Beach. We spent a day cruising on my boat — one of two that I owned on a time-share, and which I used, California-style, for impressing my business clients. Convinced this opportunity was right for me, I asked Meir to give me a few months to get the business up and running, after which I would bring him in to run the show. The son of a broker I knew told me he could find me a farm in Delano for sale and, in my enthusiasm, I wound up buying two. That was the beginning of another new direction for me, and another successful rezoning.

Now I needed investors. A few months earlier, a man named John Lederer worked in our organization. Married to Jennifer O'Neill, a young actress known for her starring role in *Summer of '42*, John had a number of contacts in the entertainment industry. He said he could supply me with about eighty of their names so I could write them a letter of introduction. With all the inquiries we sent out, we received not one response — that is, until six months later when a call came in from Chuck Plotkin, Bruce Springsteen's record producer. At our first meeting, Chuck agreed to invest $500,000. He also suggested I meet with the billionaire Pritzker family of Chicago, who, among other business interests, owned the Hyatt Hotel chain, a large investment firm, and the now defunct Braniff Airlines. The family was looking for a serious business in which to involve their twenty-seven-year-old son, Daniel. Chuck thought my new enterprise might qualify.

Daniel Pritzker had a rock group named Idle Tears, and he wanted to make an album. To that end, his parents called every qualified producer they could find. All of them assured the Pritzkers that their son had great talent, and they would be willing to produce a quality album with him for $500,000. When the Pritzkers reached out to Chuck Plotkin, however, who also agreed to do the album for $500,000, they asked him what he thought of their son's chances for success. He offered no guarantees or hyperbole. He simply told them, "It costs a lot of time and talent to produce an album, whether it sells a million records or none." Appreciating Chuck's candor, they trusted him when he said he would find something more substantial for Daniel to do with his life. I became that "something more substantial." Soon after Chuck introduced us, Daniel and I bonded immediately. Among the things that impressed him about me were my French Impressionist paintings. "My parents have a Renoir, too, and a Monet …."

I laughed at the irony, and said, "The only difference between your parents' Renoir and this one is that I copied mine from the original. My only cost was the fifty dollars I spent on the canvas and paints."

Now, Daniel was even more impressed. "Wow! Great job! I would never have caught on."

Several days later, on an invitation from Daniel and his parents, I took a Braniff flight to Chicago, by way of Kansas City. The family occupied the nineteenth and twentieth floors of a luxury high-rise overlooking Lake Michigan. Daniel's father, Jay, greeted me at the door, and escorted me through the elegant entry hall. Along the way, he informed me that his wife, Marian, was playing Nintendo in the next room. Once inside the spacious living room, I was immediately distracted by the large collection of Impressionist paintings that lined the walls. In my mind, I was comparing my copied Impressionists with these originals — only to acknowledge there was no comparison. Jay smiled at my appreciation of the artwork, thinking he had met a fellow art collector. But Daniel overheard our conversation, and spoke out. "Michael doesn't need to spend millions on paintings, Dad. He just copies them off the wall for fifty bucks apiece …."

Jay had a good laugh over that, and it broke the ice between us.

By now, Marian had joined our conversation, but, like Jay, she was skeptical about the business partnership I was offering them. Jay asked, "Why would we want to invest in milk cows?" Marian nodded in agreement.

I redirected the conversation. "More important than cows … your son has a great deal of potential, which is currently going to waste. In my new venture, I could teach him how to run a successful business … more than he could learn in four years of business school. And all I need with him is a year." Jay was quickly sold on the idea. He asked me how much money I needed and, without hesitation, I said, "Four million." He was fine with that figure, except that he wanted me to put up half of the money. We negotiated until we had a deal — 33 percent would come from me, and 67 percent from the Pritzkers.

With the funding in hand to buy a sufficient inventory, we were officially in the dairy cow business. Once we were up and running, the Pritzkers would often stop off at the Delano farm on the way to their beautiful seaside home in Southern California, just north of San Diego. On each succeeding visit, Jay and Marian expressed their delight with the advancements they were seeing — not only with the dairy cows, but with their son.

The milking was computerized at our Fresno office, which was run by expert Israeli agriculturists. I learned that the average annual yield of milk per cow was 13,000 pounds. On the lower end of the scale were the cows that produced 7,000 to 10,000, and at the higher end were those that gave 30,000 pounds. Some even yielded as much as 50,000 pounds, but they were rare. It is common knowledge that mammary glands are not created equal, whether in cows or humans. Quantity of milk varies, depending on diet, but also on heredity. A low-capacity cow gives a smaller quantity of milk when compared with the fuller-breasted variety, which tends to yield the highest capacity. So we bred the Dolly-like cows that produced 30,000 to 40,000 pounds annually, and eventually increased our average annual output to 26,000 pounds per cow. The only new requirement was the installation of larger than standard equipment to accommodate the more ample anatomy.

Breeding super-cows is a fairly simple procedure. Since a cow has a menstrual cycle similar to her human counterpart, we know that an egg drops into her uterine cavity once a month. Assuming the egg is then fertilized by a bull, it develops into a calf. Sometimes, as in human biology, the egg splits in two, and the result is identical twins. Other times two eggs are fertilized and they grow into fraternal twins. In the case of embryo transfer, instead of just one egg, up to fifty of them may fall into the uterus simultaneously. Then, the cow is impregnated by a quality bull (often valued at $2 million or more) with a record for siring quality females. Now that the cow is pregnant with fifty embryos, if left to develop the entire number, the poor creature would eventually explode. To avoid that happening, each of fifty average milk cows is assigned one of those embryos. Saline solution is injected into the womb and all fifty embryos are removed and transferred, one each, to the recruited surrogate mothers. These new mothers not only give birth to the offspring, they are also tasked with raising them. In this manner, the super-cow is relieved of the 283-day gestation period and the delivery, as well as the time-consuming hassles of parenthood. As a super-cow, she is the star of this show and is treated accordingly.

Let's assume you have a farm with 3,000 cows, which is the maximum allowable capacity due to the limited number of milking machines. And every year these cows deliver 3,000 offspring, half of which are male. That leaves a major surplus of males, since one bull is capable of servicing hundreds of cows. So, you keep 2 to 3 percent of them and 90 days later you sell the remaining 98 percent for veal. Then you have to factor in the new girls on the block, which brings your total number of cows to 4,500 — 1,500 over maximum. After singling out the lowest producers of the lot, you sell them to McDonald's. Now you have 3,000 choice cows with which to create the next generation. And the cycle continues as you slowly set the bar increasingly higher. Whereas my cows began with an average annual milk production of 13,000 pounds, eventually they were producing twice that amount — the projected 26,000 pounds. It was the same farm, the same workers, the same feed, and yet — twice as much milk. With the increased production, we began sending embryos to countries suffering a shortage of milk production. At the time, Zimbabwe was in desperate need, and with the embryos we sent them, they slowly achieved a higher yield of milk. This exporting of embryos created a profitable new income stream for our dairy farm, and allowed us to act as global humanitarians. So without additional expenses for staff or equipment, we were able to exponentially increase profit for as long as the cycle lasted.

The embryo transfer process has other potential applications. For one thing, it could be used to improve the human gene pool. But since it is perhaps too reminiscent of Hitler's "master race" concept, it has yet to find favor.

In the 1980s a major problem arose relative to increasing the milk supply: it had created a glut. Even with the lower yield of 13,000 pounds, there was an overage. With no markets left in which to sell, a farmer was out of options and had to resort to discarding the excess. Then the government stepped in, turned the oversupply into dairy products, such as cheese and powdered milk, and exported them to developing countries. In turn, the government paid the farmer for the surplus at six percent return, which was still considered a profit — but, barely. Taking a loan from the bank at seven percent interest to reinvest in the company resulted in a loss of one percent. Whatever amount of milk we were unable to sell in the private sector, we sold to the federal government. The laws may have changed in the interim, but back then it was how our country supported the milk industry. The major advantage to this surplus was that children in Third World countries reaped vital benefits to their health.

༄༄༄

Rezoning Mother Nature had become a habit with me. During the 1970s, when I was involved with Ben Gurion University of the Negev, they were studying the reclamation of desert land using innovative irrigation methods. One day I was driving through the Nabatene region and spotted an area shaped like a saucer with a large depressed center, inside of which stood a profusion of thriving fruit trees. I was amazed to see this image in the middle of a region so arid it got only three inches of rain annually, as opposed to the fifteen inches that fell on the Galilee. How could this happen? The Nabateans, who had inhabited that region for centuries, finally did the math and figured out how to make up for the deficit. They used only 20 percent of the land and allowed 100 percent of their rain to flow into the depressed center. With all of its undeveloped square miles of desert, Israel had lots of room for expanding this project, and, as a result, they became known worldwide for "making the desert bloom." Soon they were exporting their Jaffa oranges worldwide. I was inspired enough by this program to personally contribute $1 million toward its success. But, over time, with the rise in the Jewish population from 500,000 to 8,000,000, at least some of the orchards were forced to give way to new construction.

A related study used grass imported from Australia. They planted several varieties to determine the type most durable in the desert environment. This was important work, as deserts across the planet had been expanding, with one glaring exception — Israel. Australia is 70 percent semi-arid, or desert, and claims to be the driest inhabited continent on the planet. Antarctica is drier, but its human population (residing at a number of science stations) accounts for no more than 4,000 in summer and 1,000 in winter.

The Master Motivator

During this innovative detour in my professional life, motivational speaker/bestselling author Tony Robbins and I became friends, and he would often fly me to the Delano farm in his private helicopter. But although he was impressed with me, personally and professionally, he said he could not invest in my farm because of his public advocacy against dairy consumption. Confidentially, I agreed with him. "You're absolutely right," I said. "I eat very little dairy, myself. But this is Africa we're talking about. They don't have to worry about getting fat from dairy consumption. They don't get enough to sustain themselves." In the end he gave us $200,000 to $300,000 — not to feed Americans, but to help alleviate world hunger.

I had met Tony through our mutual accountant, Jim Biller. Jim was part of a large accounting firm located in Santa Monica, California. On our first meeting I overheard Tony talking to his wife on the phone, and remarking "what a great guy" he thought I was. He was married to an older woman with a few kids from a previous marriage, and they lived in one of those upscale towns north of San Diego in a home designed to replicate a European castle — not unlike my former castle in Great Barrington. For his thirtieth birthday celebration that year, Tony had professionals temporarily remove a large amount of his household furniture to accommodate the lavish party. My gift to him was a relic from Israel, a type of ancient chalice on top of which I had engraved a quotation from Rabbi Hillel. It read: "If I am not for myself, who will be for me? If I am for myself, what am I? And if not now, when?" Tony was so impressed with the chalice and the quotation that he made a permanent place for it on his mantel.

Self-made man and expert rezoner, Tony had grown up poor in an abusive household with an alcoholic mother, who threatened him with a knife when he was seventeen. That was a watershed day for him. He left home and never returned. Unprepared to attend college, he later supported himself as a janitor. Before long, and without any background in psychology, he began promoting seminars for Jim Rohn, a motivational speaker from Washington State. Through a series of infomercials and bestselling self-help books, he eventually promoted his own services as "peak performance coach." No question, Tony Robbins spoke from experience, and still does.

That he began his adult life in a low-rent studio apartment and later was able to move his family into an ocean-view hillside mansion bears testament to Tony's persistence, passion, and dedication. Today he is so successful that he has evolved into a major philanthropist, donating all the profits from his last two books to charitable causes. This is a man who has rezoned himself so phenomenally that, in elevating his own life, he has dramatically elevated others.

இஇஇ

It was in 1990 that, due to the country's milk oversupply and the steady increase in production, our profits became too small at 6 percent to satisfy the Pritzkers' accountant, who advised us to sell the business. Over the previous five years, we had rezoned the cows into doubling their production of milk. So, the business had served all of us well, including measurable regions of Third World poverty.

Young Man Makes Good

When I met him, Daniel had been a nice young man with great potential but with no business experience. A year later, just as promised, I returned him to his parents professionally rezoned. Then, in the family tradition, he went on to graduate from

Tufts University and Northwestern University Law School. These days Daniel is a highly respected representative of the Pritzker empire with a personal fortune estimated at $2.1 billion. He is still involved with music, but now as a seasoned producer. In addition, along with his wife, Karen, he runs the Pritzker Challenge — an offshoot of the family philanthropic foundation that works with the Tufts community to help grant scholarships to underprivileged minority children. I am sure his parents would be proud.

As my company was uncoupling from our financial partnership with the Pritzkers, they sent over their accountant to check the books. I had told them from the beginning how meticulous our accountant was, having been highly recommended by the discerning Meir Braun. And now the Pritzkers were about to discover how true a statement that was. Meir's cousin from Israel, who had arrived in this country without a green card, had come to work for us early on and did an exceptional job of purchasing our stable of bulls. Because he was paid exclusively in cash, the accountant kept a separate and meticulous record of every cash withdrawal that was made in his cousin's favor — both salary and expenses. The Pritzkers, in turn, were so impressed by Meir that when it was time to let him go, they asked what he would like in return for his loyalty and impeccable work record. He told them he wanted to follow in his mother's footsteps, and open a restaurant in Bakersfield, California. The Pritzkers gladly gave him $50,000 toward that enterprise, and I matched their funds. Over the years, having had the opportunity to visit Bakersfield from time to time, I learned that not only did Meir open his restaurant, but it remains open to this day and is highly successful — probably the most beloved restaurant in the city.

೧೨೨

It was earlier in the 1980s that tragedy struck my family. In our beautiful Big Canyon home one Thanksgiving evening, Arlene had an untimely heart attack. She was immediately taken to Hoag Hospital in Newport, where the attending doctor told me there was nothing to be done for her — that she was gone. She was only forty-nine. Unwilling to accept the brusque prognosis, I called the president of Cedars-Sinai in Los Angeles, with whom I was acquainted. He arranged for Arlene to be transferred to the legendary eighth floor, which was famous, and still is, for accommodating major celebrities undergoing medical treatment. For a while, the patient next door to her was the legendary Lucille Ball, but Arlene was unaware of her illustrious neighbor. Although she never regained consciousness, my wife remained in her hospital room for two years, during which time I visited with her from eight in the morning to midnight every day, and managed to conduct my business affairs by her side. To make matters easier for myself and the children, I sold the house in Newport and moved us to three adjoining apartment units a few blocks from Cedars. That was a terrible chapter in our lives, but we remain at peace with the outcome, knowing that we did whatever was possible to revive her.

೧೨೨

Summing Up

- What is the first thing to do when going into a business you know little to nothing about? Seek out experts in the field and, before investing a dime, learn all the essentials. Eventually, you will probably have the opportunity to teach others what you know. And they, in turn, will go on to teach still others. By so doing, you will become a participant in the gratifying practice of "paying it forward." The more you find yourself giving back, the more you are likely to get in return, and in all manner of ways, not merely financial. Harry Holt was one of those gracious givers who crossed my path, and so was Charlie Patrick. I was lucky that way, which is why I do my best to follow in their honored tradition.

- Few good ideas, however innovative, are immune to expiration dates. Once you have one and take full advantage of the opportunity it presents, it is soon time to start looking beyond — to the next one and then the next. Timing may not be everything, but it is generally a vital element.

- Honesty and hard work make for a winning combination. They also allow for a good night's sleep, which is never to be underestimated when you are living your life to the maximum.

෨෨෨

First comes thought; then organization of that thought, into ideas and plans; then transformation of those plans into reality. The beginning, as you will observe, is in your imagination.

~ Napoleon Hill

᷽᷽᷽

CHAPTER 13

THE BAKERSFIELD BOONDOGGLE 1991–1996

I haven't failed. I've just found 10,000 ways that won't work.

~ Thomas Edison

෯෯෯

After sitting out the real estate recession for a while, I was ready to make a comeback. Now living on the opposite coast from my early successes, I would follow my original formula in choosing the right location. That meant steering clear of properties in the midst of urban sprawl, and looking to areas with the potential for growth. Back in New York, inspired by the knowledge that IBM was building headquarters ninety miles north of Manhattan, I had moved to the area and helped to develop it for single-family and multiple-unit apartment buildings. Now, decades later, from my new home base in Southern California, I wisely targeted Las Vegas, with its zero state taxes and its potential for rapid growth. But then I rethought my decision, and made my first major mistake. Since twenty-year-old Jeremy had done an excellent job raising money for the cow business, I decided not to inconvenience him with a five-hour commute from Los Angeles to Las Vegas. So I looked to my second choice for location, which was Bakersfield — only two hours from the city, and a more manageable drive.

I found it a pleasant California city that also showed potential for growth, although at a slower pace. And, thanks to Meir, we already knew of a good place to dine.

From the outset, we did extremely well. We hired a charismatic young salesman who raised $22 million. But the $22 million turned out to be too much. Why? Because with each additional investor, profits would be increasingly thinner than initially anticipated, and individual investors would be in equal proportion disappointed with their returns. The biggest miscalculation our salesman made in his youthful zeal was promising his investors they would see profits within the first year. So, as well as he was connecting with them on a personal level, he was using a false premise to appeal to them. He had not yet become familiar with the golden rule of doing business: *under-promise and over-deliver*.

My goal in Bakersfield was to buy raw land and develop it into finished lots, which I would then sell to builders. I worked with a broker, Jim Murphy, and, in time, I had fifteen builders buying from me. After a while our salesman realized that our construction team was moving slower than the timeframe he was touting to his investors. So in order to quell their impatience, he periodically updated them with fabricated stories regarding the phases of our development process. In the first month, he would tell them we were doing the grading. In the next month or so, we were paving. And so forth. The only problem was that, in each case, his stories were a good couple of months premature. In the end, at least some of the projects finished on time. Too many of them did not.

Complicating the issue was that most of these properties were mortgaged, which prompted me in the years that followed, 2000 to 2007, to pay cash for every property I bought. No more mortgages, no matter what. I had learned this lesson firsthand in 1974, when a recession hit the real estate industry and I lost all my mortgaged properties, totaling $28 million. Fortunately, a few were free and clear, allowing me not only to salvage $2 million (as I mentioned earlier in these pages) but, because of it, to have the means with which to start over. Most investors I knew had not been so farsighted. While my good luck was entirely self-generated, the same was true when my luck turned bad.

Like with all lies, chronic perpetrators are eventually found out. When the investors discovered that our salesman had been deceiving them for well over a year, they promptly took control of the business and put Jim Murphy in charge. Then they calculated their projected loss on the properties, which came to $3 million — reimbursement for which they rightfully claimed from our salesman. In order to save the young man from a jail term, I signed a judgment for the $3 million. Each month thereafter, I paid off the debt — $100,000 at a time.

Mortified, I wrote off Bakersfield as a colossal mistake, and took off for Las Vegas and my professional future — mine and Jeremy's. As for the salesman, he got a job at a local real estate office and remained in Bakersfield.

෴

The Las Vegas chapter of my life began that same year: 1996. Not knowing a soul in a town so seemingly impersonal, even surreal, can be overwhelming and intimidating. So in times like that, when my life was essentially starting over, I would seek out those people with whom I had an inherent, eternal bond — the Jewish community. And more specifically, whenever possible, Israeli Jews. It wasn't difficult to find an Israeli synagogue in Las Vegas, nor to mingle with its congregation. Once inside Or Bamidbar (Light of the Desert) Synagogue, I chose a pleasant-looking man to sit beside for Shabbat services, and it turned out my instincts had served me well. His name was Sam Ventura, and he introduced me to a group of Russian investors, who quickly committed to underwriting my projects. Just like that. Well, not *just* like that. It took a little schmoozing and a bit of checking one another out.

With some money coming in for overhead now, I quickly leased office space and hired a couple of employees, including a fellow Israeli, David Shirit. I put David in charge of properties, as I had previously done with Jim Murphy in Bakersfield. I also installed desks for sons Joel and Jeremy. Over the years, I had gradually formed a family business with those two of my four children. David, the eldest, was never interested in real estate. His world was and remains music. Nor was my only daughter, Sharon, drawn to the business. She happily found her niche in life as a doctor's wife and mother of one son, Joshua.

Not long after my initial encounter at Or Bamidbar, I returned there and met a high-energy Israeli named Zoli Aharoni (aka Aarons). One of the most persuasive people on the planet, Zoli managed to talk me out of fulfilling my $100,000 monthly commitment to the Bakersfield investors. But once I stopped sending the checks, Jim Murphy hired an investigator to check out my Las Vegas properties for the purpose of filing an injunction against me. By this time, my debt had been reduced to about $2.5 million, plus accrued interest. So I had shown my intentions were pure. Well, at least, in the beginning.

One day a broker invited Joel, David, and me to lunch, ostensibly to meet with some potential investors. But as soon as we arrived, we found we had been set up by Jim Murphy and another investor, Rick — both active members of the Bakersfield group. Accompanied by their investigator, the two men served me with a fifty-page judgment. Since Joel had no stomach for controversy, he excused himself from the table, left the restaurant, and disappeared into the parking lot. David, who was not financially or emotionally invested in the situation, acted as a neutral observer. His one contribution to the heated conversation was, "May I order lunch?"

Timing again worked in my favor. Because the real estate market was strong, I was able to offer Rick and his co-investors 5,000 square feet of property on Paradise Road to pay off about 80 percent of my debt. I had been holding onto the property for myself in case of an emergency and, as it turned out, this was it. After confiding in Rick my reasons for having stopped payment, I found him unexpectedly sympathetic — so much so that we eventually became good friends. By the end of our encounter that day, he was in an excellent mood. He not only had good news to take back to his fellow investors in Bakersfield, he had made a $250,000 commission representing their cause.

But that was not the end of the Bakersfield fiasco. Although the investors were able to sell my property into a strong market for twice the $3 million I had owed them, they had the chutzpah to demand an additional $1 million. Their claim was outrageous enough that it drove me to court to plead my case. Yes, I won, but not without help from the attorney on the other side. He had apparently forgotten to extend their judgment against me, rendering their entire case null and void. Apparently, my incredible streak of good luck was still with me. Not as much could be said for that absent-minded lawyer.

Getting entangled in lawsuits generally involves an enormous expenditure of time, court costs, and legal fees. As an investor, you also have to be something of a lay psychologist — if for no other reason than analyzing the players with whom you become involved. I have found that no matter how much experience you gain over the years, you are always gambling in matters of trust — whether with a stranger or someone you know. *Especially* with someone you know.

છે છે છે

Summing Up

I offer the following dozen rules to live by, results of my decades-long experience. Pay close attention. One day you will likely need to act on at least one of these principles, whether for business purposes or personal.

1. Dedicate your primary loyalty to your business, over and above personal convenience and preference.
2. Don't overbuild. Purchase land out of demand, not greed. Otherwise, it could cost you in multiple ways.
3. Don't take investor money when it conflicts with your ultimate goal, which is to make the best possible profit for your investors. Their satisfaction is your major priority, or should be.
4. Treat your investors' money as you would your own. When you lose, it's their money that vanishes — but your reputation.
5. Invest in areas with ample room for expansion.
6. Never depend solely on the advice of others. You are your own best advisor, because no one knows you better, and no one is a better cheerleader for your success.
7. Perform comprehensive research in advance to ensure that the risk you are taking is relatively equal to the potential for profit.
8. Live comfortably between market cycles by eliminating your debt and building a strong financial cushion to see yourself through.
9. Never give up on a project you believe in. Not as long as you can keep it financially afloat. Sometimes it takes longer than expected, but almost invariably your patience will be rewarded.

10. Conversely, don't do anything you *don't* believe in. Sometimes your instincts are your best advisors.

11. Build in accordance with the quality of the area. But do not discount the advantages of building in a cheaper community. Regardless of income, everyone needs a roof over their head.

12. Given the choice, build multi-family units rather than single-family homes. In any financial setting, rentals tend to be more affordable and, therefore, in greater demand.

ॐॐॐ

Ignorance or forgetfulness of the law may keep a lawyer from winning your case, but not from collecting his fees.

~ Anonymous

ॐॐॐ

CHAPTER 14

OUTSIDE-OF-THE-BOX THINKING IN LAS VEGAS 1990s AND BEYOND

Thinking outside of the box keeps you from suffocating inside of one.

~ Matshona Dhliwayo

ೡೡೡ

Most of these chapters contain stories that would never have transpired without an innovative thought process running counter to general opinion.

Owing the launch of my successful real estate career to Charlie Patrick and his brilliant and generous mentoring way back in my Poughkeepsie days, I have been following his lead for years — mentoring others to achieve their goals, which are often similar to my own. My principal mentee in Las Vegas was Zoli, who credits me, among other things, with teaching him how to "think outside of the box." He caught on so well to my inventive — sometimes unconventional — ways of doing business that I eventually made him a partner on some of my projects.

What makes Zoli unique is not only his flair for creative thinking, his sharp wit, and his worker-bee mentality and persistence, but also his lifelong ability to rise above a congenital malformation of his right arm and to consistently challenge it, creatively and good-humoredly. Zoli's outside-of-the-box thinking has provided him with novel ways to use his limb that our more "normal" arms disregard. Furthermore, it has in no way diminished his social interaction or limited his ability to fully succeed in business or in his personal life.

Pay Dirt – 1996

I will never use the expression "dirt cheap" again. Here's why:

My first project in Las Vegas involved a man named Bernie Cohen from Muncie, New York. He had bought a piece of property called Woodbury Park, and took me in as a partner. When we learned that the soil on the land we now owned was "expansive," Bernie feared he had lost his entire investment. Why? Because expansive soil, when wet, is capable of damaging or destroying the building it supports. Depending on the amount of water with which it comes into contact, this type of soil is capable of breaking a structure's basement and/or its foundation. But there is a remedy — costly though it may be. To make the soil resistant enough to sustain the weight of a building, the top three feet of soil must be removed and replaced with less expansive soil. A case in point is a particular hotel on the Strip, where one small corner began to tilt. Despite the Strip's reputation for its "good dirt," this particular spot was found to be an exception. In order to repair this major oversight, the builders contacted a company in Philadelphia. Their team arrived and added materials under the foundation to secure the building and permanently restore it to its original condition.

In the case of Woodbury Park and its inferior dirt, we were quoted the cost of replacement, based on cubic yards, at a hefty million dollars. The only good news in the story was that we had gotten the land for a paltry $300,000, so we were still, barely, in bargain territory. I told Bernie not to worry about the soil and that we would work it out — although, at that moment in time, I didn't know how. Ordinarily when you buy land, you check the soil as part of the overall inspection. But because New York land, with which Bernie and I were more familiar, does not present this type of problem, we neglected to fully investigate. Back there, the primary problem for land developers was the presence of rocks, which were far easier to detect than bad dirt.

Checking the property thoroughly is a savvy investor's first task. Because he suspected our lack of experience with Las Vegas land, the seller had taken advantage and stuck us with a flawed property. So now we needed a million dollars' worth of good dirt to replace the three feet deep of bad. Costs for this "bargain" tract of land were beginning to add up in my mental calculator. In addition to paying for the dirt, its transfer by truck could realistically cost us $100,000.

Fortunately, good timing worked in our favor. While it was typical in the Woodbury Park area to deal with expansive soil, the Strip, as we know, was blessed with excellent soil with an expansion rate of one percent as opposed to our own at ten times that amount. One morning on the way to the office, Zoli drove past the construction site for the new Paris Hotel on the Strip, near Flamingo Road. He saw that the crew was digging

for placement of subterranean parking and had already accumulated enormous mounds of dirt. Fully aware of the value of
that Strip dirt and the fact that we required precisely what they
were planning to dump, Zoli parked his car and asked to speak
to the project manager. The news was far better than he had
anticipated. Yes, they would have to dispose of their dirt, and
yes, it would entail a major expense. When Zoli mentioned
that we were in need of such dirt for our nearby property at
Flamingo, where the freeways intersect, the project manager
was most receptive. He said, "I can't help you with the truck-
ing expenses, but I would be happy to pay you $100,000 to
haul off the dirt." Wait — *he* was going to pay *us*, rather than
the other way around? Although the thought had not occurred
to him, Zoli took it in his stride, and immediately struck a
deal. He couldn't wait to deliver the good news to me. This
monumental savings for us had been the result of excellent
timing mixed with situational awareness and a brilliant talent for outside-of-the-box thinking. Full credit for this strategy went directly to Zoli. And Bernie Cohen went to bed that
night a far calmer investor.

But there was one issue yet to be resolved: what to do with
the three feet of bad soil we were about to remove from our
land. Once again, good timing and creative thinking came
into play. We had another property adjacent to this that was
significantly low in soil, and it needed an infusion. So, what
more convenient place to dump the bad soil than into another
bed of bad soil? We saw this maneuver to be as harmless as
shooting someone who was already dead. What could it hurt?

In the end, I didn't make a million on this project, but I did *save* a million, which, when you think about it, is theoretically the same thing.

৯৯৯

Another project with Zoli and his outside-of-the-box thinking involved overhead power lines, which we both agreed were not only an eyesore, but an impediment to commercial development. This unsightly wiring ran directly above one section of a prime five-acre parcel that spanned the street from Flamingo to Paradise to Swenson — one long block from the main thoroughfare of Las Vegas Boulevard. The all-but-vacant land was owned by the electric company, and, while they were not in a position to sell, they offered us a sixty-five-year lease with four ten-year extensions. Now I had to convince city officials to relocate those power lines underground so that we could transform the property into an attractive location for doing business. Cities tend to respond positively to opportunities for increasing their revenue, and taxes on properties and businesses are two of the most direct routes toward that goal. After presenting our case to the city council, they easily agreed to make the power lines disappear.

Before long, we had opened a series of restaurants along that strip. Aside from an Indian eatery called Gandhi, which had previously been established on Paradise (it had never been affected by the power lines), in one corner we built a branch of the upscale Morton's, which I redesigned to resemble its popular namesake in Los Angeles. The next restaurant on our list was Roy's, which was part of a restaurant chain from Hawaii. Third and last was a franchised Jack-in-the-Box. In all, we had managed to accommodate every dining budget in town.

At first, we had failed to notice a 1,000-square-foot vacant corner of the property fronting on Paradise. But one day we took a closer look and realized its value. Because of the premier location, we were able to sublet the space for five dollars a square foot, instead of the standard three or four. What made this an especially good deal was that the cost of the land was already built into the lease agreement. The previous tenants, inadvertently or otherwise, had simply failed to build out to their maximum allowance. This is another example in which taking the time to research your property and to measure its advantages versus its drawbacks generally pays off — sometimes in significant numbers.

The lesson here is to know what you have, and make sure to maximize its full potential. Conversely, set out to recognize its failings from the start, and, if necessary, cut your losses.

ؘؘؘ

No matter how long you've been doing this work, you are never certain of the outcome. Zoli remembers how we, along with a younger partner named Sam, went to the county regarding our latest purchase of raw land, and applied for a basic zoning ordinance. In our subsequent meeting with the city council, our application was turned down, which in theory represented a loss of $1.5 million. By then it was seven o'clock in the evening, and we headed from the parking lot to a casino for dinner. Sam lit up a cigarette and looked suspiciously at Zoli, who was laughing. "Why are you so happy?" he asked. "You lost." Sam was too inexperienced to realize that winning and losing were a constant in this business, and in order to survive either outcome you had to take it in your stride. As this particular scenario turned out — six months passed, and we got the entire lot of eighty acres approved for rezoning, after all. What accounted for a change of heart on the part of the city council? Possibly, it was the fire truck we donated to the local firehouse. It seemed logical to us that a firehouse should have a fire truck — which, oddly, theirs did not. We had merely given them what they needed, and they reciprocated in kind. Again, you see in action here the immutable principle of getting what you want.

The moral of this story is that, win or lose, you are advised to accept the hand you are dealt. Make light of it, learn your lesson, and move on. If you neglect to follow these simple rules, you will never fully enjoy your life, no matter how successful you become. And keep in mind, success is not measured by how much money you make, but how much satisfaction you give and receive along the way.

It Pays to Advertise

These days, billboards represent big business. Technology has infused them with elements capable of driving more traffic than the papered panels of the past. Some billboards stream video and others are illuminated with an internal light system that makes them come alive at night.

Few of my projects in 1998 took less effort and yielded a higher return that a tiny piece of those five acres — an over-looked section at the corner of Flamingo Road and Paradise. Like the thousand square feet that had gone unused by its previous owner, this corner, because of its miniscule size (no bigger than a dining table for two), would have remained untapped by most entrepreneurs. But Zoli is far from "most people." In this instance, he and his outside-of-the-box thinking came up with an idea that, with little to no time or effort, made us a cool million dollars.

Its value was in its location — along the road from McCarren Airport to the LaMar Convention Center. Zoli decided, small as it was, the space offered enormous potential for a billboard company, since it could be used to accommodate a three-sided billboard facing three well-trafficked Las Vegas streets.

To determine the land's worth, I put in a phone call to a reputable billboard company in North Carolina. After hearing what we had to offer, they gave us a bid of $700,000. I was so shocked and embarrassed by the figure that I robotically said, "Oh, no!" Fortunately they took my reaction literally, and immediately raised their bid to $1 million. Before they had time to retract it, I said, "Sold!" In such rare instances, it's that easy to make a million dollars — but I wouldn't count on it.

ﻉﻉﻉ

Illuminated billboards use a series of advertising images instead of a fixed one. This allows them to rotate in multiples, each one appearing for a set period of two seconds before rotating to the next, and then to the next. The process works on the same principle as neon lights, which also change every couple of seconds — and on traffic lights, which are changed through a timer from green to yellow to red. Although animated streaming video represents the latest in billboard technology, it is legally confined to city limits, as it would naturally pose a safety risk on the open road.

There are laws governing outdoor billboard advertising in relation to indoor sales. With indoor advertising on your premises, you are not permitted to also advertise on a billboard outside. Also, you may only promote your own project, including, if appropriate, yourself. I researched the statute that governed the issue, and found a convenient gray area, which we justifiably exploited. We proceeded to advertise whatever we sold inside, including various whiskeys and soft drinks, and, in turn, our suppliers offered us discounts for the privilege. For example, designer sunglasses might have cost us five dollars apiece, but if we were to advertise them on our billboard, the company would give them to us at no charge. Imagine how much deals like that increased our bottom line.

Shady as it sounds, this is considered a legal loophole. As a bar owner, you are allowed to install an illuminated sign, make a proposal to your suppliers, and, based on the density of traffic, wind up making as much as $2 million a day. For example, were you, as the bar owner, to buy $200,000 worth of a popular soft drink, once you advertise it on your billboard, it costs you the deeply discounted rate of $25,000. The same holds true for assorted alcoholic beverages, including top-shelf whiskeys, and all the rest. Is it any wonder that licenses to sell alcoholic beverages cost a small fortune and require you to sign onto a waiting list?

Currently, Zoli is developing a public bathroom in which sponsored ads for soft drinks pay him $1.99 every time someone comes in to pee. Only if the individual stays for no longer than two seconds is there no charge. Length of stay is tabulated through a scanning system. And this same process works in various other areas of business. Capitalizing on this new trend, a computerized service headquartered in Europe supplies digitized advertising around the world. This would be a perfect partner for Zoli's new profit center in restrooms, where the public that goes to pee also has the benefit of checking their pulse, their BP, and their blood glucose. And, of course, their urine and stool.

Doctors beware! You may soon be operating out of a john.

❧ ❧ ❧

A few years after Zoli and I developed the five acres along Flamingo, the City called to say they were now prepared to sell that parcel along with four others from various locations. Zoli and I showed up at the auction with the requisite deposit check of $250,000, hoping to finally purchase the land we had been leasing for so long. All seemed to go well enough; we won the bid and we were already celebrating inside of our imaginations. But, not so fast. All throughout the auction, there had been a somber-looking man and his equally dour wife sitting next to us. They never spoke to anyone, not even to each other, and they especially ignored the auctioneer. I had noticed the man was scribbling something in a small notebook and occasionally showing it to his spouse, but I suspected they were just exchanging idle comments to pass the time. Then, after all the properties had been auctioned off and the winners were bursting with excitement over their new acquisitions, the auctioneer made a deal-breaking announcement. He said the City was prepared to void all of the winning bids should any one among us be willing to purchase the entire collection. In that precise moment, dead silence filled the room. And that was when my somber seat neighbor raised his hand. Rather than make his intentions known early on, he had apparently chosen to sit unobtrusively calculating the market value. Then, when it reached its peak, he quickly factored in a minimal addition to the total, and made his transformative bid. And that "minimal addition" was just enough to sabotage every one of the former bids — Zoli's and mine included. Not an honorable way to do business, but unfortunately for the rest of us, not illegal. What added to the irony was that now, instead of writing our rent checks to the electric company, we were forced to pay this devious individual on a monthly basis. Moving into the future, the disheartening incident would be an ongoing reminder of the lengths to which some people go to achieve their aims — in our case, not only for Zoli and me, but for all those bidders who left the auction that day, empty-handed and angry.

No matter how experienced and savvy you are going into a negotiation, this is one of those occurrences that keeps you humble and on your toes. Soured by this outcome, Zoli and I eventually sold our lease to a Persian/Iranian named Isaac Norman, who paid us about $4 million in an up-trending market cycle, which rated in banking terms as a 4 percent cap. For those of you unaware, the cap (capitalization) rate dictates the price for selling any income-producing property, including a lease. By the cap rate you pay, you can anticipate the amount of your income. If I were to buy a property for the purpose of making 5 percent, I would pay 20 times the figure, because that amounts to 5 percent interest. The difference between, say, a 4 percent cap rate and a 5 percent, or even a 10 percent, is the interest you are willing to pay as the buyer. As the market improves, the cap rate decreases — sometimes to as low as 3 percent. Conversely, in a bad market, the cap rate increases, generally up to 10 percent. The positive side of a bad market, and one to keep at the top of your mind, is that it often provides an opportunity for higher than usual profits. But, as with all great opportunities, it also increases your risk.

"Contaminated" Vacant Land and Buried Cars

During the same period that Zoli and I leased the five acres along Flamingo, we discovered a nearby piece of property on Tropicana, between the Orleans Hotel and Home Depot. Having previously been run by an auto repair business, it carried an automotive zoning. It also carried a stigma as victim of a pervasive rumor that the land was contaminated by — well, nobody knew. Maybe by oil spill — maybe something far more macabre. And that persistent rumor was primarily the reason it sat for twenty-five years waiting for someone with foresight to buy it and restore it to life. Unlike its potential buyers of the past, Zoli and I were unconcerned about what was buried beneath the surface. As Zoli so practically said, "It could have been a dead body for all we cared — of course, with all due respect to the deceased." What mattered to us was that we liked what we could see, which was a bargain price and an excellent location for attracting business. So we bought the property and then brought in an expert from Los Angeles to perform a soil test at a cost of $2,000. We even used an ultrasound device to check out the unidentified rectangular box buried beneath the ground. In the end, we solved the mystery. What had been hidden for a quarter of a century was neither an oil spill nor a dead body, but a collection of defunct automobiles. After digging out the cars, we rezoned the property for commercial use (C2) and developed it for a shopping center. We had planned to install a Big Ben bar and had already built the foundation when we discovered the site was located less than the requisite 1,500 feet from an elementary school. So, instead, we built an uncontroversial coffee shop that we called Catch a Cup of Coffee — designed in the shape of a large coffee cup with an inserted teaspoon. An innovative technology we were using for the first time allowed us to charge first-time customers on their credit card. Then on subsequent visits, the transaction would be done automatically, through license plate recognition. Customers liked the convenience, and we liked to please.

One of my favorite notions was to build a hot dog stand with a dollar sign for a logo and a catchy name: In Dog We

Trust. Then the market collapsed, and so did my plans for the hot dogs — which remain, of course, on the back burner.

ରେ ରେ ରେ

Summing Up

Never assume anything, and be fully aware of the potential negatives connected to any purchase, regardless of what a good deal it seems at the outset. In fact, a "good deal" by definition should raise your level of suspicion. Unknown factors can be expensive when they hit, and they often arrive in multiples — cutting into your profits, if not eliminating them completely. Ever since that incident with expansive soil, the first thing I do is check out the dirt on every property that catches my attention.

Learn how to determine and apply the cap rate, which is the ratio of Net Operating Income (NOI) to property asset value. That means a property listed for $1 million generating an NOI of $100,000 would equate a cap rate of 10 percent (or 10 percent cap). The cap rate is a most valuable tool when comparing it to similar properties at a given point of time — especially in terms of asset type and location.

Steve Jobs, founder of Apple and outside-of-the-box thinker and innovator, once said: *Here's to the crazy ones. The misfits. The rebels. The troublemakers. The round pegs in the square holes. The ones who see things differently... the people who are crazy enough to think they can change the world are the ones who do.*

ରେ ରେ ରେ

One who takes the road less traveled earns the rewards most missed.

~ Matshona Dhliwayo

৵৵৵

CHAPTER 15

THE PLUNDER FROM DOWN UNDER 2003

... If you work hard enough and assert yourself, and use your mind and imagination, you can shape the world to your desires.

~ Malcolm Gladwell

ৡৡৡ

Brad, my long-time accountant, does not drive — so he does most of his commuting around Beverly Hills on foot. During his travels, he meets some interesting folks. On one particular day in 2003, he stopped for lunch at the Luxe Hotel on Rodeo Drive, and met a young real estate developer from Melbourne, Australia. Victor had come to the United States to tap into the hot Las Vegas property market, and Brad wasted no time in introducing us.

Having done his research on prime properties, Victor narrowed his search to the two long blocks on the Las Vegas Strip between Sahara and Charleston, and soon placed several lots into escrow on an adjacent street. For one of the sites, he designed a high-rise condominium, which he called Liberty Tower. It was to be comprised of 140 units, most of which he pre-sold to members of the gay community. Unfortunately, he ran out of time, as the market began to show serious signs of weakness. The bank that had committed to lending Victor the construction money interpreted the market signals, as well, and abruptly voided their transaction. With nowhere else to get the funding, Victor was forced to return all deposits and cancel his sales. In the aftermath, the realtors sued him for their perceived lost commissions, but he prevailed in court.

I purchased the property from Victor with plans to call it the Monument, in honor of my deceased wife, Arlene. In keeping with my theme, I hired the Australian architect Eugene Marchese to redesign the building with its 22 stories and 236 units into the curvaceous shape of a woman. But in the wake of the resounding market collapse of 2008, I was forced to put my plans on hold. While the crisis was felt nationwide, it hit particularly hard in Las Vegas, where the prices had been rising faster than in most U.S. cities and, therefore, were far more vulnerable to the drop. Within a short period of time, Las Vegas real estate lost, on average, 80 percent of its value. To this day, even in recovery mode, it has not yet retraced its previous highs. Fortunately, I was able to keep renewing my approvals, and I am still holding onto the property, along with my cherished dream for the Monument.

Prior to the downturn, Victor had the corner of the Strip at Sahara tied up. He was waiting for the right buyer to show up and provide him with a handsome profit on his investment of $2.5 million. It took him several years to find an offer he was willing to accept, but eventually Walgreen's provided the magic number ($4.7 million), netting Victor a tidy $2.2 million profit for his patience.

Victor's timing turned out to be perfect, as he barely missed the precipitous drop in prices that followed. Then, with the market reversal in its early stages, he lost the incentive to remain in the U.S., and flew back to Melbourne a richer and happier man. Before he left, he told me he would later set out for India, hoping to repeat his good fortune there. Judging from what I knew of him, I can only assume he accomplished his goal.

Around the same time I purchased the Liberty Tower from Victor, I signed a contract with a motel owner next door to buy his property for $5 million. When it was time to close the deal, however, the seller backed out. He said the property was now worth $10 million. We went to court, and I lost, which turned out to be a blessing for me, since, following the crash, the motel's value plummeted. It is currently being offered at $2 million, with not a bargain hunter in sight. The lesson here is, sometimes you *can* win for losing.

I experienced a reverse scenario with another property a couple of blocks north, which I had contracted to buy for $3 million. The seller refused to sell for the same reason, that its value had increased. This time around, the courts found in my favor, but it turned out to be no favor at all. As of this writing, the property continues to languish — which only goes to prove, you can also lose for winning.

One of my real estate deals in Las Vegas involved Bob Stupak, who was considered by some to be the greatest huckster in a long line of notorious Las Vegas hucksters. Stupak had a history of gambling and bad real estate investments that gained him a less than stellar reputation — even in a town filled with disreputable people. But when he finally built the innovative Stratosphere, with its 1,049-foot tower, its roller coaster ride, and its NASA-inspired rocket ride, his detractors became less vocal. That is, until the enterprise went south and lost $100 million in stock value. Fortunately, Stupak preserved his legendary sense of humor, which could not be said for his luckless investors.

ෂ්ෂ්ෂ්

Money can't buy happiness, but it can certainly get you a better class of memories.

~ Ronald Reagan

ෂ්ෂ්ෂ්

CHAPTER 16

MAKING GOOD MONEY IN BAD CYCLES
2009–2016

A banker is a fellow who lends you his umbrella when the sun is shining, but wants it back the minute it begins to rain.

~ Mark Twain

ৡৡৡ

In 2003 I had paid $1.125 million for a two-and-a-half acre parcel of land at Arroyo Grande and Horizon Ridge in Henderson. By June 2006, with the real estate cycle in its final months and my timing stunningly accurate, I sold the property for $3.4 million, garnering a hefty profit of $2.275 million. It wasn't long thereafter that the bottom dropped out of the market with major reverberations.

A bad market is often an outstanding opportunity for those with a solid track record to buy, as they say, "with both hands." Certainly that technique worked for those savvy investors who had foreseen the 2008 crash as much as two years earlier, and set aside enough cash to pick up the pieces in the aftermath. Investors who felt the worst of the downturn were among those who had previously enjoyed the best of it — on its way up. This was particularly true in Las Vegas, where, as

I mentioned previously, prices had escalated so rapidly and so astronomically, it seemed they would never come down — which, of course, was a strong indication that they *would*, and soon.

The bursting of that bubble, which affected over half of the United States, technically began in 2006. Housing prices peaked early in the year, and then continued their fall into 2007 — reaching new lows until 2012. On December 30, 2008, the Case-Shiller U.S. National Home Price Index reported the largest price drop in its history. Then, as with all cycles, the market began its long climb back toward normalcy, but not without leaving serious devastation in its wake.

I was there from the beginning to see it happen. Multi-million-dollar properties lost up to 90 percent of their value, virtually overnight. My own real estate was not immune to the drop, either — declining by an average of 65 percent. The difference between other investors and me was that I was free of debt and in a strong enough position to ride out the recession. Being debt-free is always crucial. You may recall I had learned that lesson many years before when caught in a similar position. A lesson is generally worth the price you pay for it, as long as you apply it accordingly.

By 2008, foreclosed properties had overrun the banks with their unwelcome presence — many the result of relaxed mortgage standards. While the upside of a mortgage is that it allows an investor to pay for a property over time, the downside is the inherent risk, should its revised market value fall below its mortgage value. In such a scenario, it makes no financial sense to hold onto it, and that's when the bank acquires it by default. But for all those mortgage holders who lost their homes in the crash that year, there were the well-prepared holders of cash eager to buy them up at a steep discount. I was one of them.

In total, during the course of that real estate debacle, my investors and I bought twelve foreclosed properties from the bank for a few cents on the dollar. One property that I knew to be valued at $2.25 million, once it foreclosed, became mine for $300,000. Two years later, I sold it for $900,000. If I had chosen to wait it out, eventually I would have been able to sell it for its original price. But I was satisfied with the 300 percent profit, and was ready to move on. Even then, there was one big opportunity my investors and I missed. Next to our property, where the 95 meets the 215, there sat 60 languishing acres where a company named Triple Five — builders of the Mall of America in Minneapolis — had planned to build a huge shopping center, the much anticipated Mall of Las Vegas. But the company was caught off-guard by the market drop and the bank foreclosed on its $27 million mortgage. The bank, in turn, sold the property for $6 million to a developer friend of ours, who put the property on the market for upwards of $30 million — so far, with no takers. Slowly, my friend is reducing the price, and, once he agrees to settle for a more realistic figure, he will probably find a willing investor in the comfortable neighborhood of $22 million.

Since 2012, Las Vegas real estate has regained much of its former strength, but still has a way to go. The market will move slower this time around, but likely with more solid footing.

If you aren't already invested, the next turnaround might be the right one for you to double your dollars. In the meantime, use this interval to gain knowledge, and maybe even seek out a mentor.

Getting Investors to Yes

It is never an easy task to win the trust of potential investors. You have to assure them they are not likely to regret their decision, while never guaranteeing them, either, which would be wholly unethical. These people worked hard to acquire their capital, and they are naturally more worried about losing it than they are excited about making a profit. However, they know they have few places as attractive as yours in which to park their money. Certainly, getting a measly percentage or two from the bank is hardly a satisfying solution. And, barring any runaway inflation scenario, the prospect of receiving anywhere close to the 16 percent returns of the 1970s is pure fantasy.

Investing in raw land is rock solid, even more so than investing in a house. Land is 4,000 miles deep, and all yours — all the way down to the center of the earth. It's as real and as permanent as this planet it lives on. And it could yield you a profit of 50 to 100 percent or more, whenever you decide to sell. This is an important point to drive home to potential investors.

Two additional facts with which to ease your investors' concerns:

1. If the project in which they are invested is not attached to a mortgage, which none of mine is — and I hope

yours won't be, either — there is no way to lose. You are safe from foreclosure as long as you are paying your property tax, which is usually calculated at one percent of the value of your investment. Of course, if you neglect to pay for three or four years, the city or county has the right to take it over and sell it at auction. At that point, you would be forced to accept whatever the winning bid offers, minus your tax obligation. Chances are that figure will be lower than market value.

2. Compare this rock-bottom risk to investing in stocks, which could nosedive to zero over a volatile weekend, leaving you with nothing more than a worthless paper certificate. Land is physical, material. In even the grimmest of scenarios, assuming the city permits, you could pitch a tent on it or live out of your car.

In normal times, investing in raw land is a three-year commitment. If the land is being rezoned, the process can take about six months. And then all you have to do is sell it in its original condition. Easy, and consistently rewarding. However, if you want to build on the property, factor in a three-year process prior to sale. A third option, once you've finished building, is to use the property for rental income. Every one of these scenarios is a winner. The one you choose should depend on personal choice and/or circumstance. However, if you are looking for a financial vehicle that makes money for you while you sleep and even for a lifetime, rental property is about as good as it gets.

During the downturn, I bought a house in Las Vegas for my young partner's mother, who had a FICO rating of 850, and was therefore able to borrow the money at a low 2 1/2 percent interest rate. Through my broker, Terry Barone, she bought a 3-bedroom house for $80,000 that would normally have sold for $300,000. Her intention from the outset was to rent it out. I suggested she buy six others in that tract under those excellent conditions, and she would never have to work again. But she chose the conservative route, saying, quite understandably, she wanted to see how this one worked out. Fortunately, it worked out well, but by the time she felt comfortable buying additional properties, the market prices had risen above her price range.

I cannot overstate this: For those of you interested in a comfortable retirement, early or otherwise, owning income property is one of the best investments you can make. Since downturns are inevitable, don't concern yourself with having missed out in recent years. Over time, opportunities will present themselves again — and again. One of the keys to reducing costs as an investor is having a strong FICO score. For tips on how to elevate yours, check out one of the numerous websites dedicated to your cause. One of the most popular at this moment is CreditKarma.com, where, at no charge, you will be able to check your current score regularly, and read valuable tips on how to improve it. Also, check with your bank, as they may offer the service as a benefit to their depositors.

While downturns vary in time and intensity — from mild to manic — the formula never changes: Buy low. Sell high.

Since that advice is easier to impart than to practice, I would suggest you modify the formula to a more realistic equation: Buy when your market analysis dictates it's at a low. And sell when it dictates a high. You should also allow your instincts some input. Combining both strategies, you stand a good chance to win. The main variable will be, by how much.

Land values may decrease every once in a while, temporarily, depending on those inevitable cycles. But the ultimate direction is always up. Patience is generally required, but it is likely to reward you. This is especially true when you buy land in a dense and/or prime area, where the general population wants to live and work. The equation I use for investing in raw land is based on pure logic: *People multiply. Land does not.* This formula certainly applies to Las Vegas, where an increasingly large influx of people is expected to vie for a limited amount of primary land well into the future. Developers will be forced to work the available property in order to accommodate these newcomers with homes, apartment dwellings, commercial real estate, hotels, etc. It's a simple matter of supply and demand.

According to *Forbes*, Las Vegas has greatly recovered from the recession and now ranks as the eleventh fastest growing metropolitan area in the country. While it still has one of the highest foreclosure rates and largest inventories of vacant homes, it is attracting new people and businesses at a healthy rate. The Las Vegas-Paradise metropolitan area is expected to grow from 1.988 million in 2012 to 3.32 million by 2042. At an increase of 67percent, this will account for one of the largest population booms in the United States. It's all in front of us, and so are the enormous opportunities.

Buying and Selling Property for Profit

If you are not a professional, but have a property to sell, you are advised to list with a reputable broker or organization. Currently, zillow.com and craigslist.com are among the highest ranking of internet sites. There is also loopnet.com for commercial properties, lotnetwork.com for selling lots, and a number of websites and blogs offering tips on the buying and selling of real estate. When you sign with a licensed broker, you are committed to paying a brokerage fee, which is normally 5 or 6 percent. I find it is best to go with someone you have reason to trust, rather than to sell or buy on your own. Even though you will be saving on commissions, you may significantly miscalculate the value of the property and therefore stand to lose considerably more.

It is also essential to take along an appraiser when evaluating a property — just as you would a mechanic if you were checking out a previously owned car with a private seller. He or she can check for flaws as well as other matters of which you may not be fully aware, such as need for an easement. It is also imperative you do a soil test. You never know what may lie beneath the surface of any property you investigate. I already discussed with you what Zoli and I discovered on the land we bought next to the Orleans Hotel.

Before you enter the market, establish as best you can where you stand in the current cycle. On average, cycles run seven years up and then seven years down, but they can vary enough to throw you off course. Naturally, the bottom of the market will suit you best for making the greatest profit, but how can you be sure you've hit a true bottom? Bottoms can be tricky. That's why some of them come to be known as "false" bottoms or "double" bottoms, even "triple." But with so much to gain, there's also the inevitable risk to factor into the equation.

I have not only bought at the bottom of a market, which was easy enough to determine in 2008 — I have also bought at the top, thinking there was still some growth to come. Successfully second-guessing these markets takes as much luck as it does savvy. In 2007, when Las Vegas prices still seemed headed skyward, I bought four acres of land for $4.3 million. It didn't take long after to realize I had bought at the uppermost peak. Currently, that property remains unsold at an asking price of $2 million. But the story is not all bleak. Averaging out my transactions from that period, I found I did outstandingly well. Of the twelve properties I bought just prior to the downturn, I made only one mistake — and as long as I refrain from selling it into a weak market, I will eventually retrieve its full value.

ఆఆఆ

Summing Up

Despite the inevitability of the market cycle, with all its twists and turns, there are ways both subtle and obvious to tap into its inner workings through the people around you. One day in Los Angeles, I was staying at a hotel, and had entered the elevator with my luggage. The valet asked me if I were a real estate builder. I said I was. He smiled and said, "I had a hunch. I just invested in three homes here, myself."

And then I knew. When lower wage earners are buying into the market, it signals that anyone with a dollar to spare is already invested. It reminded me of the often-told story of Joe Kennedy (JFK's father), who recognized the peak of the stock market in 1929 after his shoeshine boy offered him stock tips. Another financial wizard of that period was Bernard Baruch, whose narrative just before the Great Depression reads as follows: "Taxi drivers told you what to buy. The shoeshine boy could give you a summary of the day's financial news ... An old beggar who regularly patrolled the street in front of my office now gave me tips ... My cook had a brokerage account and followed the ticker closely. Her paper profits were quickly blown away in the gale of 1929."

❧❧❧

The art is not in making money, but in keeping it.

~ Proverb

❧❧❧

CHAPTER 17

DEVELOP YOURSELF AS A DEVELOPER

Buy at the sound of cannons. Sell at the sound of trumpets.

~ Nathan Rothschild

❧❧❧

Buy when there's blood running in the streets.

~ Baron de Rothschild

❧❧❧

Both pieces of advice boil down to a wise and long-held observation on contrarian investing. When the masses are acting out of fear during a crisis, they tend to sell out at any price. Since crises are built into the system, as is predictable human behavior, it is safe to say that however stormy a situation on any given day, eventually the sun will shine through. And that's when those who keep their cool while others are losing theirs tend to prosper.

This is not a course in real estate development, as that would take another, more comprehensive book — one that has probably been written many times over and revised and updated regularly.

If you are serious about following my lead, I recommend you take a course, whether at your local community college or online. You can even start by reading books written by well-known experts with platinum track records. In addition, the internet comes to the rescue as the ultimate source for virtually every facet of knowledge. Just be sure to verify data before you grant it your trust. You might decide to visit the popular biggerpockets.com, which is a real estate investment network eager to get you started, including a free downloadable book called *The Ultimate Beginner's Guide to Real Estate*. Considered by some to be the Warren Buffett of real estate investing, John Schaub recently published *Building Wealth One House at a Time*. There is so much information out there, I suggest you follow those instincts of yours and narrow down your options. Raw land? Single-family homes? Multi-family units? Commercial real estate? Rezoning? Buying? Selling? Building? Leasing? Flipping? Figure out the pluses and minuses pertaining to your circumstances and preferences, and slowly test the waters.

For example, if rezoning is the specialty that most attracts you, pay close attention to those who have perfected their skills within that niche. Then, too, you might choose to start with one niche, and transition to another. Alternatives abound, but focus is advised.

Your Beginner's Guide to Becoming a Real Estate / Rezoning Guru

Start out with one thing in mind: location. Speaking from experience, it's better to pay more for a piece of property in a good area than to take a chance with a cheaper property in a region with a number of potential problems. Of the thirty-five pieces of property my investors and I currently own in Las Vegas, every one of them is in a prime area. We have nothing in the boondocks or surrounded by cheap homes. But, as I've already mentioned, there is room for such investments, as well.

When you are checking out a property, be sure to investigate all the land in the adjacent areas. You should become knowledgeable about any near-term construction plans with the potential to affect your locale — good or bad. For that matter, any news, whether local or global, can directly or indirectly affect the value of your property, and that can even include an earthquake in Turkey or a sugar shortage in Cuba.

Visit your location of interest at various times of day and evening, even the dead of night. And weekends, too. You want to be aware of noise levels, street crime, neighborhood activity, parking, and so many other elements that come into play on any given street, residential or commercial. You want to know what the schools are like, the shops, the police and fire departments, access to roads, freeways, hospitals, emergency clinics, and so forth. Are there animals in the area that tend to bark incessantly at night? What about sanitation services? Are the streets and alleys clean and safe? You need to be fully aware of these things and more because they might impact the value of your property. And don't forget your potential buyers' right to such information, as well. The more you reveal to them of your research, the greater their reason to trust you.

Location is not only about the street or neighborhood you choose, but even the city — since you may be willing to invest in an area an airline flight away from you. Naturally, an absent landlord acquires an additional set of problems, but when the property offers a number of advantages, such as price and value, it may be worth considering. You could always hire an experienced project manager to help you run and maintain the property.

One of the major reasons I have never chosen to buy and/ or rezone in the middle of urban sprawl is that the red tape is much redder and the application process much longer and more frustrating. In a city like Los Angeles, for example, the rezoning process can take as long as two years to complete. And after all the time and effort you put forth, you may find the profit — assuming there is any — doesn't come close to compensating for the pain. In such a case, you essentially wasted those two years and temporary access to your money. Worse still, you may have hit a glitch in the middle of the process that completely derailed the project.

A particular commercial building currently going through a long and excruciating approval procedure in an affluent Los Angeles community has been in limbo for over two years, despite the fact it has met every city ordinance and criterion without controversy. Detractors — mostly no-growth neighbors — have found assorted excuses to sabotage the project, including a small adjacent business that has been earmarked for historical preservation.

By contrast, the City of Las Vegas encourages builders to develop the area, so they accelerate the process down to a few months and increase your chances for rezoning approval.

Negotiations are done on a more intimate level. The number of people you deal with is fewer and the incentive to help you is greater.

If you don't have access to the ear of a city official, then do your own sleuthing through the local papers. Your chamber of commerce can be helpful, so you are well advised to join. Aspiring to their board of directors is also a smart move, as a great deal of reciprocity goes on among its members. The majority of them tend to be lawyers, bankers, money managers, real estate developers, hoteliers, restaurateurs, and high-end retailers. Membership can be costly in time and money, but can more than compensate in benefits — the most important of which is that the organization exists to serve the business community. That means their interests are also yours.

Although I had performed well enough in Bakersfield, where I initially expected to duplicate my earlier successes in Dutchess County, I could have done better. In retrospect, my sons and I bought too much land and depended on too many mortgages. But we learned from the experience and in 1995 moved on to Las Vegas, which was the right place to go at the right time for development and growth. And we're still there. For the following decade, before returning to Southern California, I called Las Vegas my full-time home. Currently I divide my time between both places. For me, it's a perfect balance.

かかか

Summing Up

Whether a newcomer to the field or a seasoned professional, it helps to be tuned into upcoming trends. Let's say a huge corporation is headed your way. That is potentially excellent news, because it automatically translates into an increase in new jobs, higher real estate values, and a greater demand for new housing. This holds true not only for the company directly, but for the subsequent influx of sub-contracting companies. It also means an increased need for schools, hospitals, and cultural venues, among other essential facilities. I moved to Dutchess County early in my career because I had learned that IBM was setting up new headquarters there. The fact that I gained early access to that information, understood the ramifications, and acted on the knowledge was highly instrumental in igniting my budding career. Just as I had anticipated, the new IBM operation increased the demand for homes in the region for the foreseeable future. I speak from authority, since, over the next fifteen years, I built 1,000 of those homes.

ৡৡৡ

Buy land, they ain't making any more of it.

~ Mark Twain

ৡৡৡ

PART TWO

INTRODUCTION

❧❧❧

In Part One of this book you learned why I consider rezoning one of the most effective ways to multiply profits in any real estate transaction, while also reducing financial risk to a minimum. As I explained, rezoning is not about increasing the market value of an inferior piece of property. It's about taking an already valuable entity and, by enhancing its functionality, automatically endowing it with greater potential into the future.

Decades ago, the process of rezoning was used only by builders when needed in the development of a real estate project. And then I came along and reset its parameters for larger financial profit with no additional work. As you already know, back in the 1960s I found that all I had to do to rezone a property was convince three members of a city council to vote in my favor. In this instance, I unwittingly discovered it took nothing more than a London Fog raincoat and a TV set. Later on, in a different circumstance, I gave a real estate investor the painting from my office wall, which he had greatly admired. You may also recall that on one early project I extended the property line of a group of justifiably hostile neighbors in exchange for their approval. Ultimately, we all came out ahead. This is the cardinal rule for the successful rezoning of land — learn what the community wants, and find a way to give it to them.

In Part Two I talk about the potential for life essentials, unrelated to land. For most of my eighty-seven years, I have lived what most people would consider a charmed life. I have enjoyed the satisfaction of professional achievement, intellectual challenge, respect of my peers, financial independence, love of family and friends, good health, spiritual contentment, and the deep satisfaction of giving back to the world. Conversely, I also experienced the tragedy of war while still a teenager, the loss of my young wife to a stroke, the occasional reversal in business and finances, and betrayal by people I trusted.

I will now attempt to pass along the benefit of my experience, my research, and my hopes for the future as well as my views for exponentially rezoning and raising the stakes in some of the most essential aspects of existence. These include: health, humanity, and spirituality, all of which contribute to the sum total of sustained happiness. They have done so in my case. I also emphasize the importance of mentorship by providing examples of how the process of rezoning people — transforming them from functional into exceptional beings — presents them with opportunities to conduct the rest of their lives at an optimum level.

In addition, I opine on the Apostle Paul, who fundamentally rezoned my own Jewish religion for the purpose of appealing to an international population of nonbelievers. Paul was so successful in his mission that he transformed his modified model of Judaism (a kind of forerunner of the Jews for Jesus movement) into the phenomenal faith the world recognizes today as Christianity. From my perspective, therefore, Paul earns the #1 position on any list of Best Rezoners of All Time.

Lastly, I suggest a new form of rezoning I call "pre-zoning." Applied to children, pre-zoning refers to the discipline of seeking out their specialness, mastering it over time, and permanently integrating it into the fabric of their lives. Not every child is born a prodigy, but every child is endowed with unique innate abilities and passions that, when properly nurtured, may be practiced at such an elevated level that they often negate the need to rezone. But most of us have not been that fortunate.

At various times in your life, you will have an opportunity to rezone yourself or another person, place, or thing. If you've never knowingly done it before, you may be unsure about pulling it off. But I say you can — you can do most anything reasonable you set your mind to doing. You can take a known entity, and make it bigger, better, and more beneficial than you ever thought it was meant to be. And be sure of this — in your capable hands, it *was* meant to be.

ॐॐॐ

CHAPTER 18

REZONE AND GROW SUPER-HEALTHY

Health is the greatest gift, contentment the greatest wealth,
faithfulness the best relationship.

~ Buddha

ॐॐॐ

Wouldn't it be nice to know that however good, even outstanding, our current state of health, it could only get better from here, or at least no worse — for the rest of our lives? And we would not have to lift a finger to help it along. No expensive dental procedures. No inconvenient doctor visits. No uncomfortable colonoscopies. And, for that matter, no diets, no vitamin pills, no exercise regimens. Nor would any junk foods or colas be restricted from our menu.

Issues of longevity tend to occupy more of my thoughts with every succeeding birthday, which is the primary reason I am inspired to write this chapter — to share my perspective on the present state of healthcare and evaluate its future. My life and yours may depend on it. I have always emphasized the importance of fitness and nutrition in my daily routine. But decades ago, with the sudden loss of my beloved Arlene, I became more vigilant than ever about taking proper care of myself. Following her untimely heart attack that Thanksgiving evening long ago, I learned first-hand that however well we are feeling at any given moment, circumstances can shift irretrievably within a matter of seconds. Therefore, we would do well to prepare for such an occurrence and, by our lifestyle, help lower the risks.

In addition to maintaining your current state of health, I will show you how to rezone it for greater durability, strength, resilience, immunity, and resistance to the ravages of age, which are already starting to unravel by the time you reach adulthood. Studies vary, but the general consensus is that our brain cells begin their natural decline from our mid-twenties, and our bodies follow suit over the decades to follow. Unfortunately, most of us are feeling so great in those earlier years that we tend to believe we will ever be so. Self-delusion is so much easier to maintain than a nutritious diet and a sound exercise regimen.

But before we start talking about super-health, let's address ground-level reality and what I consider "reasonable expectations."

Tripping Over Your Ego

If you want to keep your health intact, you must pay it the attention it requires and adhere to its strict demands. But be aware that no matter how much energy you expend on keeping fit as you grow older, you cannot expect the same sterling standards from your body as you could at twenty.

Until I was fifty, I felt invincible — as though I could live forever, untouched by the frailties of age. But once I passed that major milestone, it didn't take long before I noticed little things going wrong. At first, it was nothing more than a minor loss of physical strength, particularly in my legs. Wisely, I had no intention of ignoring those early warning signs or retreating into a state of denial. So, I started going to the gym three times a week and I hired a trainer to be sure I was exercising correctly and getting maximum results. After a few months of rigorous exercise, including pushups and workouts on a stationary bike, I was rewarded with an increase in muscle mass, which allowed me to add new weights to my strength training. In the process I lost an unwanted sixty pounds.

Then one day at the gym I grabbed the attention of four physically fit women in the midst of their workouts, one of whom commented skeptically, "I'm impressed. How much are you pushing?"

"Six hundred," I said, falsely modest.

Said another, "Come on. The four of us together can't push six hundred."

I said, "Really? That's nothing. I can do a whole lot better than that."

"Show us."

"Bring it on," I said, my male ego out of control.

And they did. A couple of them took on the task of adding weights to my barbell until they totaled 900 pounds. Then they stood back, arms folded, and dared me to lift. I had no choice but to try. But the moment I grabbed hold of the overstocked iron, I felt a click in my spine and a simultaneous shift in my abdomen. And that was the moment I had a fateful encounter with vanity. It was also the instant I set up my back for the

painful and chronic condition of spinal stenosis, which would
not show up until years later. The same would be true for my
strained stomach, which dislocated on the spot and, over the
years, traveled toward my lung, where it currently resides —
causing me intermittent bouts with shortness of breath and
chronic pangs of regret.

When I first felt the symptoms in my spine I called on
a doctor, who diagnosed me and gave me a "one-time-only"
injection. The discomfort was gone for months, leading my
physician to believe the treatment was permanent. But a year
and a half after the initial injection, the pain returned, and
I had to convince him to repeat the one-time-only shot for
a second round. This time the pain was gone, it seemed, for
good — or, at least until many years later when I resumed
my strength training with gusto. In the interim, no one had
bothered to warn me that lifting weights was strictly forbidden for someone with my condition. I had to learn that on
my own, albeit with disastrous results. But on the bright side,
and as I illustrated earlier, there is no more powerful way of
learning a lesson than through misfortune. The moral of this
part of the story is that if you choose to ignore medical warn-
ings, this weight-lifting cautionary tale of mine should cure
you for all time. As I write this, the pain remains a constant
in my life, although I have gotten somewhat used to it. As
for the displaced stomach, I am assured it presents no serious
problem — unless I eat a bite or two too many at mealtime.
An elective surgical procedure exists to cure the condition but
I am inclined to be skeptical.

So here I am, a man who has been lucky most of his life, enjoying excellent health and often testing it to the extreme. If you derive any one thing from this book, make it this: *Never take your health for granted. Spoil it rotten and baby it — and it will love you for all time. Baseball great Mickey Mantle once said, "If I knew I was going to live this long, I would have taken better care of myself."* Who over fifty cannot relate to that one?

ॐॐॐ

Caveat: This chapter is not for anyone with serious pre-existing medical conditions, as those must be addressed by the best physicians available to you in their field of expertise. Then, once your basic health issues are under control, and with the approval of your primary physician, you can reread this chapter for recommendations on how to rezone to a higher level.

Anyone with super-health as a goal should reach beyond the highly accessible information available today, the ABCs of it, and also check out alternative treatments, procedures, processes, protocols, solutions, studies, and scientific journals. And then, when indicated, take action accordingly. But always be sure to get a highly professional second opinion, and, if necessary, a third. The internet is filled with enough disclaimers and detractors on any medical issue to provide a balanced argument for or against. Don't be confused or distracted by what one or the other tells you. Remember, even the so-called experts are known to make serious, sometimes deadly, mistakes.

We certainly know this to be true of Big Pharma — and you don't want to become one of their sad statistics.

ৡৡৡ

You Are Never Too Young to Slow Down the Aging Process

Early in life, when you are most likely to enjoy excellent health, that is the best time to begin your personal program of prevention by monitoring mind and body on an ongoing basis. Unfortunately, the standard motto for most members of the younger generation is — no pains, no worries. The problem with that philosophy is that most of our health's greatest enemies are already working unseen and unaccounted for deep within the estimated 37.2 trillion cells of our body. By the time they finally announce themselves loud enough for us to hear, much of the damage has already been done. It is worth noting that, according to scientific data, the human body plays host to about 100 trillion microbes on any given day. Simple math tells us, therefore, that the majority of our body's cells are of a non-human variety. I don't mean to imply that all of these uninvited guests are guilty of foul play, but in a population that large, there have to be a few million or so with less than noble intentions.

We will not discuss the common cold or flu, except to say that these are mostly treatable and short-lived, and come and go with few, if any, consequences. What we are going to review here are the basics for keeping well, long term, while outward signs are still pointing in that general direction.

The recommendations below encapsulate an amalgam of information currently available in a variety of health books, speeches, websites, newsletters, and blogs—with just a dash of common sense and logic tossed into the mix. Quotations and accreditations are kept to a minimum, as most of the conclusions are widely accepted and derived from multiple sources. The goal of this chapter is not to overwhelm you with data and reference material, but to provide you with an overview of what to expect in the field of healthcare so you will be informed enough to take full advantage.

Health Essentials

1. Sleep six to eight hours a night, but no more than nine. Get ready for bedtime by turning off your electronic devices an hour or so before switching off the reading lights and pulling up the covers. That includes everything from TV to iPhone to iPad to Kindle to your laptop computer — and anything else with a plug or a battery. When you hit the pillow, it also helps to turn off your mental activity and think simple focused thoughts, like counting sheep or numbers backwards from 100. I sometimes resort to counting U.S. presidents or my favorite movies of all time. But why limit the categories? This method works as well with car models, state capitals, song titles, and ice cream flavors. Whatever topic strikes your fancy is fair game. If you are feeling particularly tense, reach for your bottle of essential oils, like lavender or chamomile, and inhale

deeply and repeatedly three or four times — until you feel relaxation coming over you like a warm blanket. But if all attempts at slumber fail after the first twenty minutes, concentrate on the sound of your breathing — the repetitive process of inhaling and exhaling. A busy mind is not always likely to turn off on cue. You may have to nudge it along with focus, calm, and repetition.

2. Upon arising, drink at least eight ounces of water, which helps to awaken your organs and energize your body. Throughout the day, remember to drink another glass every hour or so for healthy hydration. In summer months and during or after exercise, increase your intake. Remember, coffee and wine tend to dehydrate the body, so adjust the volume accordingly. A good rule of thumb is to drink half of your body weight daily. So, for example, if you weigh one hundred twenty pounds, that's sixty ounces of water on your to-drink list every day — or just under eight eight-ounce glasses. Not all fluids in your daily quota must be in the form of pure water. Such liquids as tea, lemonade, and fruit juice are viable alternatives.

3. Walk, don't run. Take a brisk walk before breakfast every morning or in late afternoon. If you do both, even better. Among other things, morning is for the absorption of Vitamin D and afternoon works toward a good night's sleep. Although thirty to forty-five minutes of daily physical activity is better, ten to fifteen minutes

is acceptable, particularly when repeated three or four times within a twenty-four-hour period. In between, especially if you are sedentary during the day, get up on your feet at least once an hour and walk around — even if it's just to the bathroom and back. Of course, the greater the distance to your bathroom, the better. Also, anything you are now doing seated that can be as easily done standing up, opt for standing. During the day, if you have errands to run, force yourself to park at the farthest end of the lot or the next block away. When practical, do those errands on foot.

Over the past few years, it has become popular among fitness devotees to count their number of daily steps and make sure that (rather than the average of 3,000) they add up to between 7,500 and 10,000. That's a lot of your day to spend stepping, but think of the things you get done. Devices like Fitbit make it easier for you to keep track of your steps, as they do the counting for you. Even your iPhone monitors your physical health. No doubt technology is on the job and looking out for you 24/7. More about this later.

4. Destress and think positive thoughts. Find at least fifteen minutes a day to seal yourself away from humanity and luxuriate in some "me time." Use those precious minutes for meditation, spiritual protocols, or simple exercises proven to calm your body and mind, such as yoga or tai-chi. A bonus period like this each day gives you time for focusing on new ideas or rethinking old

ones. You already know the impact of positive thinking on your state of happiness. The same holds true
for your state of health. Whenever you are faced with
a negative thought, stop it dead in its tracks and break
the cycle by switching to something positive — however random it might be. For example, you might be
stressing out over your anticipated tax burden for the
year. Well, that's not going to cheer you. So, instead,
send a STOP! signal to your brain and replace it with
one in which you are finally getting your well-deserved
job promotion or selling your inspired memoir for
a million-dollar advance. See how that works? With
enough practice, and by minimizing your risk for heart
attack, cancer, stroke, hypertension, depression and the
like, you could be adding more healthy years to your
lifespan and making it a lot more fun. This is where
you get to apply your vivid imagination. As I mentioned earlier, lavender and chamomile also work wonders. Never underestimate the power of aromatherapy.
Why else are we advised to "smell the flowers"?

Given the high stress levels of my daily work routine, I am grateful for my mind-and-body regimen,
which consistently guides me to calm and tranquility,
and assures me a good night of sleep.

5. Eat balanced and nutritious meals. Eat less salt. Eat
    less!!! If you are overweight and want to lose some of
    those pounds, the best way to diet is simply to eat
    smaller portions of what you generally consume — and

to eat more slowly. It takes about twenty minutes for your brain to get the message from your stomach that it has reached its capacity and craves nothing more. But if you are eating faster than your stomach can relay the message, you are sending it surplus supplies. And that is one of the major reasons you tend to gain weight. Besides, eating slowly allows you to experience the process with greater satisfaction. You actually get to taste and savor the food you are taking into your body — and that's where the fun of it comes into play. Here, as in many aspects of life, it's not the quantity that counts, but the quality. For example, as much as you may delight in devouring a huge helping of chocolate cake, studies have shown that the first two bites are the ones that yield the most pleasure. Every bite after that is merely adding calories while simultaneously decreasing the level of gratification. And since few of us stop after the second bite, we rarely take notice of the diminishing returns.

If you have to cut back on your favorite foods, there is no need to feel like a martyr. Plenty of low-calorie recipes exist that will allow you to eat enough to satisfy your cravings until your next meal. And, to sweeten the deal, if you are following the rules, you are allowed to reward yourself once or twice a week with an otherwise "forbidden" food. Now, that doesn't sound so draconian, does it? And it gives you something to look forward to.

Use the standardized food pyramid found on the internet and in most diet books to keep yourself on track, so that, on a daily basis, you are sure to ingest the proper amounts of protein, calcium, fiber, starchy carbohydrates, "good" fats, etc. Having protein for breakfast (eggs or a protein shake, for example) is a good way to power up your energy for a productive day ahead, especially if you add fruits, such as blueberries or raspberries, to the mix. Protein also satisfies your appetite sufficiently until lunchtime, so that you aren't tempted to placate mid-morning hunger pangs with a fistful of sinful snacks. A handful of nuts (raw walnuts, almonds, cashews, pistachios, etc.) offers a healthy alternative. Lunch can replenish your energy level with veggies, salad, cheese, lean chicken, fruit, or some variation of your own choosing. Dinner: repeat a variation of lunch, but, if you like, in slightly larger portions. A motto worth remembering: the best exercise you get at mealtime comes from pushing yourself away from the table.

Choose especially nutritious foods, such as: sources of fiber found in whole and cracked wheat, plus beans and legumes, avocados, salmon, lean chicken, broccoli, nuts, sweet potatoes, dark green leafy vegetables, quinoa, and most fresh fruits, particularly berries, but also grapes, apples, cantaloupe, and watermelon and at least a dozen others. Be sure to find a way to add garlic, onions, and olive oil to the mix, as well as assorted herbs such as ginger and turmeric, which are as tasty as they are health-giving. And the latest flash from nutritionists is that healthy fats are vital to your health. These include: red meats, whole milk, cheese, and even some types of bacon. So there is no longer a reason to deprive yourself.

These suggestions are but a small sampling of the many dozens of delicious staples that make eating healthfully a relatively easy chore, even for those who are currently hooked on sugars and refined carbohydrates. A good rule of thumb is to substitute seasonings for sugars, which are easily as satisfying. Do your research for items that are best enjoyed organic, as their non-organic counterparts may be doused in dangerous insecticides, without which you may live longer and healthier. Also, be careful of certain foods that contain poisonous or hazardous components absorbed from their environment. For example, certain fish are considered more toxic than others, and those are generally the bottom-feeding shellfish that live in heavily polluted waters as well as the larger fish that harbor plastics and other refuse from deeper ocean waters. But this warning doesn't mean to imply you should eliminate all fish from your diet. Just be selective about the ones you choose for mealtime. Also, if you are not getting enough fish oils in your diet, take a supplement of 1,000 to 3,000 mg a day. Also be sure you are getting all your necessary vitamins and minerals.

A good barometer for determining how well your body is absorbing the nutrients you send it each day is to get a blood panel taken at least once a year at your physician's office or their go-to lab. You don't want to come up on the short end of such health essentials as the B vitamins, C, D3, E, magnesium, calcium, and on down the list. You might also check out K2, which is purported to have amazing health-giving properties, including protection for your bones. Also, there are many minerals you may not even know about, but which your body requires to run efficiently.

If you are willing to experiment with fasting, you may be doing yourself an added favor. Studies have shown that going without food for twelve hours straight (some say sixteen) may yield major health benefits to your mind and body. This is easier than it seems, and merely requires finishing dinner by the same time that, twelve hours later, you will be having breakfast. For example: conclude dinner by seven in the evening and eat nothing until seven the next morning. See? As I told you — easy. Eventually, you might want to work up to sixteen. But one milestone at a time.

6.   Be social. If you are married, make it the best marriage you can — as it may have the power of adding days, months, and years to your life. Keep in mind, this person you married is someone you once thought you could never live without. In case you lost that feeling along the way, seek out a way to retrieve it. There's a

strong chance you can, you know. But, if you are alone, you can still enjoy your freedom — and your intimacy, too. Never discount the importance of close family ties, solid friendships, and productive professional alliances. Communication is essential, as are mutual support and self-expression. Use the word "love" (as in "I love you") with discretion, but on a frequent basis. You want to show appreciation to the people within your universe on a regular basis. Chances are, they appreciate you back and like being reminded that the feeling is mutual. Hugs are also known for their health benefits, and — just a reminder — there is no such thing as a hug overdose.

Another health-giving relationship is the one you have with a pet. And if you don't yet have an animal to pamper, you might give it serious consideration. For all the inconveniences they may impose, their benefits to you and your sense of well-being are potentially far greater. They even force you to take a few more of those essential steps each day, and they're always available for a health-giving hug.

7. See your doctors and dentists for routine visits, and whenever you are experiencing symptoms for which you have no logical answer and which tend to persist, don't delay setting up an appointment.

8. Go off the grid once in a while and indulge your inner rebel. If you are conscientiously caring for your health, you deserve an occasional break. If the mood and the

opportunity strike, follow your heart's desire. Go to
bed at daybreak. Sleep in for an entire morning. Keep
off your feet all day long. And, go ahead — eat a hot
fudge sundae or half a pizza. Do whatever it is that
gives you instant pleasure. Rewards can act like goals
in that they give you moments of delayed gratification
after a long and arduous workweek.

No matter how diligent we are, or how superior our DNA,
there are no lifetime guarantees on the state of our health.
While it is normal for the human body to remain disease-
free, there are thousands of bodily functions that are capable
of going haywire, even under our radar. So, always be on the
alert, expect the unexpected, and, when necessary, take appropriate action.

The Transitional Age of Medicine

There is good news and bad about the way healthcare is being
delivered in the United States and in other developed nations as
we move deeper into the twenty-first century, with its increasing dependence on technology. At the same time, we are leaving behind what has been called The Golden Age of Medicine,
which, according to popular opinion, ended a few years before
the twentieth century came to a close. Those years were considered golden for good reason. Despite a greater knowledge
today of how to keep patients healthier and a vaster number
of them alive, there were many benefits to patient care that
have become increasingly scarce. And those of us old enough

to remember have valid reason to miss them. Forty or fifty years ago, physicians were far more likely to treat their patients as whole human beings. They knew the names of our spouses and pets, greeted us at social events, and sometimes visited our homes. They had what was called "bedside manner" and they genuinely cared about our well-being. For them, as well as for us, it was decidedly personal.

What they didn't have in such magnitude were the bold and potentially life-altering advancements that are headed our way — some of which are already here. No matter how old we are, we all want to live long enough to reap the benefits of those technological innovations that will be reconfiguring human lives: diagnosing diseases, replacing damaged body parts, and rendering "miraculous" new cures and treatments that we are just barely learning about. The older we get, and the more we bear witness to the inevitability of disease and old age, the more meaningful and hopeful we are about the future of medicine.

Considering the deteriorating reputation the healthcare industry has suffered in recent years, they are now trying to reverse public perception by instituting a "put people first" motto, which mates the human body with precision machinery. And rather than replace the patient's choice in decision-making scenarios, technology will simply assist them in the process.

Rezone Your Health to Super-health

A few of the following recommendations are so essential at any stage of life and at any time in history that I repeat them from the previous list of essentials.

- Become well informed on the general condition of your body: what makes it work, what encourages it to break down, and how to reassemble or treat it for greater functionality and endurance. Create an inventory of your specific body parts, assess their damage or potential for damage, and seek ways to prevent, treat, and/or cure. On a regular basis, make particular note of those things that might be hinting at trouble ahead: hair, brain, scalp, neck, spine, teeth and gums, eyes, skin, throat, thyroid, esophagus, lungs, heart, veins, arteries, blood vessels, pancreas, liver, kidneys, stomach, small intestine, large intestine, gender equipment, musculature, endocrine and hormonal systems, bones, tendons, cartilage, ears, nose, sinuses, hands, fingers, toes, feet, knees, legs, thighs, as well as all the rest. With so many parts to the whole, some are bound to elude you. So for ongoing reference, I recommend you seek a comprehensive diagram of the human body. One of the many places to find one, or a series of them, is at www.innerbody.com.

- Get regular checkups with doctors, dentists, and specialists you trust and respect and, when necessary, seek out referrals for the best in their fields.

- See your dental hygienist at least twice a year. And, in between, maintain good hygiene by brushing thoroughly no less than twice a day, and flossing or irrigating at least once. Unhealthy teeth or inflamed or infected gums can cause damage that extends way beyond your teeth — sometimes making a direct and deadly beeline for your heart or your brain. Make it difficult, if not impossible, for bacteria to have their way with you. You're way bigger than they are.

- Don't worry about looking like a hypochondriac. So-called hypochondriacs are those patients who most effectively advocate for their body and act on its behalf. In the process, they may seem funny to some, but, as it usually turns out, they are the last ones laughing.

- Don't believe everything you hear. On the other hand, don't be too quick to discount anything. What sounds inconceivable today may seem ho-hum routine by next week.

- Never take "I don't know" for a final answer. Medical professionals don't know everything, nor should we demand they do. Since there is just too much for any one person to assimilate, we sometimes have to take it upon ourselves to find solutions as well as the proper clinicians to administer them.

- Don't automatically accept your doctor(s)'s diagnosis. Maintain your quest for answers until you are fully satisfied with what you hear. If you must change doctors a dozen times in the process, so be it.

- Learn. Learn. Learn.

- Keep active. There are reasons you were given a pair of legs, and, unless they are seriously impaired, it is your responsibility to use them well and often. And that goes for the rest of your body. As we age, unless we are scrupulous about physical activity, we tend to lose muscle mass and all the attendant functions that define physical strength and independence. As I mentioned earlier, we need to face the reality that what we had in the past will not always be there for us in the future. At least, not to the extent it once was. But, from a positive perspective, this only means you have an opportunity to take on the challenge your body is offering you, and ultimately claim victory. Besides being active during the day, you are best served by adopting an exercise protocol that appeals to you on a personal level. This should be not only something you enjoy doing, but that involves the whole body. For some, it's bicycling, which, while it seems to occupy the majority of moving parts, may still fall short in certain areas. Identify those deficits and practice supplemental routines to compensate. This advice applies to any activity, including gardening or dancing or swimming or anything that keeps you moving and engages your body. There are any numbers of exercise routines from which to choose, including: pilates, strength-training/weight-lifting, interval training, resistance movement, stretching, stair-stepping, and just plain walking. Choose one or a combination of those that best address your body's needs and integrate them into your daily schedule. Yes, it takes time you would otherwise use for something else. But, no, that is not a valid excuse. There are a number of minutes that go wasted during the course of your day. Seek them out, rearrange a few of your more flexible habits, and you now have the requisite time to restore the body you once took for granted.

Warning: Before beginning any exercise regimen, be sure to get your physician's approval. I repeat: Before beginning any exercise regimen, be sure to get your physician's approval.

- Keep positive. Good thoughts are generally followed by good actions, which are the cornerstones of good health.
- Maintain your self-esteem. This is the trait most deeply motivated toward your personal well-being.
- Like yourself. Make an inventory of those qualities that you believe make you a worthwhile human being, and refer to it on a regular basis, lest you forget.
- Look good. The better you take care of yourself on the outside, the more likely you are to look after yourself where it doesn't show. And that is where your self-esteem resides.
- Think good thoughts. And, if you are so disposed, practice the power of prayer. Your mindset is forceful enough to energize your entire being and aid you in any healing process.
- Smile. Laugh. Repeat. See the funny and beautiful sides of life all at once, and often. Laughter heals. Besides, it's fun.
- Be purposeful. Have a goal. And once that is accomplished, have another. Infusing your life with

permanent meaning gives you the motivation to get up in the morning and remain on track.

- Maintain a close community, personally and professionally. Mutual support is life-affirming and life-giving.
- Create a two-way path to affection and love, and travel it daily. Love can never be underestimated nor overly expressed.
- Rid yourself of negative people. They are not likely to change, and they will only tear you down in their drive to build themselves up.
- Do things for others. The more you feel needed on this earth, the more likely you are to stick around.
- Have passion in all things.
- Live the cliché: Do the things you enjoy and enjoy the things you do.

What if something gets you down and you have to fix it on your own? For every condition on earth that needs mending, there is also a natural repair tool. If it hasn't yet been discovered by medical science, it's only a matter of time until it is. With the right attitude, a dogged persistence, and a never-say-die attitude, you have the best chance of surviving your condition and putting it out of its misery. This is a classic case in which knowledge is power — maybe enough to save or lengthen your life. Proactivity is the name of this game, so stay alert. Healthcare is rapidly shifting from labor-driven and technology-enabled to one that is digitally driven and human-enabled.

This is my personal preference, as it puts you back in the driver's seat where you belong, and where you are provided with plenty of professional assistance along the way.

The Future of Medicine and How it Will Help You Live Longer and Healthier

Technology is driving us into a world we hardly recognize, but one where the healthcare industry is a major beneficiary — and that includes you, the patient.

Let's check out a few of the innovations that, should preliminary studies prove their efficacy and result in their being approved, will be waiting in the wings to improve your health or maybe one day save your life.

- Health sensors, implants, and other smart devices will surround us at every turn — whether at home, at work, or in transit. We will not only have instant access to the database on our health, we'll be able to transmit it to our destination of choice as well as receive a timely response. This innovative process will save time and money for both patient and healthcare provider. For the rural population of America, it will be seen as a significant boon and a welcome equalizer.

- Within the next decade or two, nanotechnology will have developed devices to successfully treat patients on a molecular level. Physical conditions, including matters of dentistry, will be candidates for any number of new protocols. This could mean the end of cavities as well as cancer. How's that for progress?

- Until recently, coronary artery blockage to the heart was treated by the insertion of metal stents, which remained forever in place. These stents often caused problems for subsequent surgeries or treatments, sometimes resulting in complications such as blood clots. Now, a biodegradable version has come on the market for the 600,000 patients who receive this form of treatment every year. Made of a dissolvable polymer, these new stents are naturally absorbed by the body within two years, eliminating the dangerous risk factors of previous versions. This is only one of the many advances that will eventually eliminate heart disease as our #1 killer.

- Cellular immunotherapy is an important weapon in the fight against cancer. The process requires the removal of a patient's immune system T-cells, which are then reprogrammed genetically to seek out and destroy tumor cells. So far, studies of blood-related cancers, such as leukemia, have reported a 90 percent rate of remission. Still in its infancy, this approach is on track to stunt and replace the practice of standard chemotherapy.

- Liquid biopsies will soon make cancer diagnosis and treatment as easy and effective as a simple office visit. In Israel, they are now snuffing out breast cancer over the course of a lunch break.

- Ketamine, a drug traditionally used for anesthesia, is being demonstrated as an effective treatment for severe depression, often yielding results in the first twenty-four hours.

- As the population ages, the number of dementia cases, including Alzheimer's, is expected to rise proportionately. The good news is that a number of studies are reporting early success with drugs shown to slow its progression. No cure yet, but there is significant reason for hope. The drug trazodone, already approved for treatment of depression, appears to stop the dying of brain cells — a major hallmark of the disease. Trazodone has already been used to treat late-stage dementia and is now being considered for early-stage patients. A second drug, dibenzoylmethane, is already in trial, showing similar results. It may be no more than two years before we know whether the work being done with mice will be similarly effective with humans. In such a scenario, dementia patients will have one or more of these drugs available to curtail their mental decline, while perhaps allowing them to hang on long enough for a permanent cure. Currently, there are multiples of studies being performed on this issue, and no wonder. The implications are — no pun intended — mind-boggling.

- In 2011, new 3-D printer technology was able to produce a human kidney, ready for transplantation. And the success stories have already begun. The first human kidney transplant using this technology took place in Ireland in 2016 on a three-year-old child, who might otherwise have had to spend the rest of her life on dialysis. This is excellent news, as it holds the potential to revolutionize the organ transplant industry and resolve the serious shortage of donor human organs. Current delays are running as long as two and a half years, and over 7,000 people die every year while waiting for an organ transplant. With the 3-D hardware already in place, what has been missing until recently was a kind of "ink" with which to replicate human organ tissue. According to Erik Gatenholm, co-founder and CEO of CELLINK (www.celllink.com), that need is currently being addressed and resolved. The first 3-D heart transplant surgery could now be as close as six years away. In conjunction with other companies, CELLINK is also doing research on the engineering of hair follicles to cure baldness and on artificial skin to aid burn victims — with even more remarkable applications to come. The potential for bio-printing is enormous, including the extension of the human lifespan. The greatest current downside to this technology is cost, which, as with all new technologies, will likely decrease considerably as volume and availability come into play.

- Soon we will be able to get all the medical advice we need from a virtual doctor visit via our smart phone. Surgeries will, in many cases, be made without an incision, even without a surgeon — as robotic technology will more frequently take over. Other innovations are working to cure blindness and cancer, and the list will gradually lengthen to include as many maladies as are known to exist in the human mind and body. Most likely, our pets would be next in line to benefit. After all, they are one of our best defenses against ill health.

• According to www.tasciences.com, telomeres are "the caps at the end of each strand of DNA that protect our chromosomes, like the plastic tips at the end of shoelaces. Without the coating, shoelaces become frayed until they can no longer do their job." When DNA strands are damaged, our cells can no longer do their jobs, either. What keeps telomeres healthy is a protective enzyme called telomerase. But as cells divide, the availability of the enzyme is reduced, and that is when the damage is accelerated, resulting in even further shortening of our telomeres and the aging of our cells — a major factor in our overall life expectancy. How to prevent or minimize the damage is the question. A partial answer lies in the most basic of health advice, which is to stop smoking, lose weight, reduce stress, exercise more, and eat a healthier diet — one that is high in anti-oxidants, such as berries and artichokes. There are also vitamin supplements that purport to preserve telomere length, including the usual alphabet types: C and D, which preserve telomere length; D, which also promotes telomerase activity;

and carotenoids, etc. Supplements are readily available over the counter, as well as online. Do a little research, as you may want to include these in your growing daily regimen.

- Stem cells are another important determinant of health and longevity. Research being done on this topic represents the potential to regenerate and repair damaged tissue. One of the great benefits of mesenchymal stem cells (MSCs) is their natural ability to transform into bone, cartilage, and fibrous tissue, making them a natural partner in therapies for such conditions as Parkinson's, cancer, diabetes, osteoarthritis, and joint injuries.

Before the turn of the twenty-first century, research on human stem cells involved a deeply moral controversy over the use of fetal tissue in stem cell transplantation. But since that time, according to an October 11, 2017, article by Theresa Phillips for www.thebalance. com, "promising developments in other areas of stem cell research might lead to solutions that bypass such ethical issues." Because the destruction of blastocysts (fetal tissue) is no longer required, these new developments could help win more support from those who were traditionally opposed.

Stem cells can already be employed to replicate any cell in the body, and may one day be used to grow entire organs or cure diseases, such as (as I mentioned above) Parkinson's and diabetes. According to a March 28, 2017, article by Anne Grapin-Botton and Joshua Brickman for *Science Nordic* (http://sciencenordic.com), a research trial in Copenhagen multiplied donor fat cells inside four machines known as bioreactors, and were then injected into heart patients, who had run out of other options. Results were highly successful. This is another area of research that bears watching, and will likely impact the future of healthcare.

Immortality, or Pretty Darn Close

According to the World Health Organization (WHO), there are over 10,000 diseases attributable to the occurrence of just one error in your DNA. And by a simple act of modifying the genetic code in your body, an enormous undertaking that medical scientists are diligently working on, you will be able to zap virtually any disease from your body, erasing it forever from existence. And that includes the most feared and fatal diseases of all.

British-born and Cambridge University-educated (1985), Dr. Aubrey de Grey is an author (*Ending Ageing: The Rejuvenation Breakthroughs that Could Reverse Ageing in Our Lifetime*) and biomedical gerontologist dedicated to repairing the effects of aging, which he considers the ultimate disease, and which, once conquered, according to the doctor, will result in life expectancies of a thousand years or more. A thousand years may not be tantamount to living forever, but, after the first five hundred or so, it may feel like it.

Dr. de Grey is one of the few scientists today whose goal is to prevent aging rather than to merely slow it down. Cofounder of SENS Research Foundation, Dr. de Grey states, "We are developing a new kind of medicine: regenerative therapies that remove, repair, replace, or render harmless the cellular and molecular damage that has accumulated in our tissues with time."

As a patient in this brave new world of man-meets-machine, it is your job to remain ever vigilant about medical breakthroughs and how they might affect you in your never-ending drive to preserve and improve your health.

I, for one, am excited by the prospects. Stay tuned. And, in the meantime, do your research.

Summing Up

In the decades ahead, it is up to us to show our bodies the respect they deserve for making it possible for us to exist. Our evolving healthcare system will do the rest as it continues to yield increasingly positive, even seemingly miraculous, results. In the best of all possible scenarios, our life expectancy may double or triple or more, leading us to face Dr. de Grey's firmly held thesis on immortality. It would also force us to address the ultimate moral question — will this Planet Earth have the resources to sustain an ever-growing population? And if not, how can technology make up the difference? It seems we are beginning to see how. Just recently, a 3-D printer delivered up a fake hamburger. While it had all the prerequisites for sustaining life, it lacked the authentic taste. In fact, it was completely devoid of taste. However, in a case of emergency or when fed to a starving population, it could mean the difference between life and death. Besides, before long, technology will have advanced that tasteless burger to the point where it might be succulent enough to win a culinary award.

In the meantime, eat wisely, exercise liberally, think positively, and love passionately. Your lease on life may soon be renewed.

And, for once, ignore Mark Twain's advice. (See below.) He lived in a century when your local dentist was also your barber and your anesthetic was a strong slug of whiskey. Think of how far we've come, and where we are yet to go. I am in awe of the possibilities, which is why I am taking this opportunity to share a number of them with you.

ৰৰৰ

The only way to keep your health is to eat what you don't want, drink what you don't like, and do what you'd rather not.

~ Mark Twain

ৰৰৰ

CHAPTER 19

REZONE FOR HAPPINESS: PART I

If you want happiness for an hour, take a nap;
If you want happiness for a day, go fishing;
If you want happiness for a year, inherit a fortune;
If you want happiness for a lifetime, help someone.

~ Chinese Proverb

ॐॐॐ

Every one of us has known happiness in our lives — whether for an hour, a day, or a year. Sustaining it for a lifetime, however, that takes a dedicated mindset and a purpose-driven life. A life lived with intention.

In psychologist Viktor Frankl's 1946 memoir, *Man's Search for Meaning*, he chronicled his experiences as an inmate at Auschwitz concentration camp during World War II. Under the most oppressive of circumstances, he applied a psychotherapeutic method he called logotherapy to find meaning in life — which ultimately accounted for his survival. The protocol involved identifying a purpose to feel good about and then focusing intensely on that outcome. Frankl believed that one can be poor and chaste, and yet be happy. However, without meaning, no one can achieve that state of bliss, regardless of circumstances. "Only when the emotions work in terms of values," he wrote, "can the individual feel pure joy."

I've been on the trail of happiness all my life and, despite the occasional rainstorm, I've enjoyed a good measure of sunshine. Here's why. Through a process of elimination, I found lasting happiness — not by discovering what it *is*, but by deducing what it is *not*. For instance, I know happiness doesn't come from material things alone or a position of power, since some of the unhappiest people in the world are wealthy and powerful. I also know it isn't derived from love alone, because love is constantly changing, not always in my favor. I won't seek it in my state of health, either, which, like love, is subject to changes over which I have limited control. The true formula for happiness, I believe, includes a positive mindset, close relationships, and a grateful attitude, but none of these is the defining ingredient. And it's that defining ingredient we're going to discuss here. If you are going to incorporate it into your life, and I urge you to do so, you need to know precisely what it is and how to make it work for you.

According to the 2017 Harris Poll Survey of American Happiness, only one-third of Americans consider themselves happy. I hope you are among that small percentage. If you are not, this chapter might inspire you to exponentially increase your odds.

えええ

You are born. You live. You die. And, somewhere in between, the thoughts cross your mind — why am I here? What is the meaning of my life? What makes me truly happy? You know it has to be more than going to school, making a living, getting married, raising a family, and every other traditional milestone along the way.

In 1926, wealthy Scottish whisky distiller Thomas Dewar shared his theory on the subject, and garnished it with a witty twist.

We are all here on earth to help others; what on earth the others are here for, I don't know.

The late Lord Dewar is not remembered for his philanthropy, although he did create awards for a sprinkling of sporting events. However, by sharing his insightful, if not cynical, observation nearly a century ago, he created a strong set of guidelines for the rest of us to follow. We are *all* here on earth to help others. That means that, at one time or another, those "others" are likely to help us back. It doesn't take a great deal of money — in most cases, none at all — to perform a single act of kindness.

My periods of greatest happiness have always been the result of doing something for others who were unable to do it for themselves. Whenever you perform a selfless action or noble gesture, you have positively affected some person, place, or thing, which then goes on to affect another person, place, or thing. And on it goes, ad infinitum. You can ponder this subject all your life, but the simple formula is this: by giving to someone or something, you are given something in return — a sense of worth. That sense of worth provides incontrovertible evidence that you make a difference — that you matter. And knowing you matter showers gushers of happiness in your direction like nothing else on the planet.

Regardless of how long you walk the earth, by the time you are ready to leave, you want to know that in some measure you have left it at least a little better for having been here. An act of kindness is all it takes.

That act of kindness can be as simple as helping a handicapped person down a flight of stairs, or as complex as being a first responder to a neighborhood fire or a rescue operation following a natural disaster. But a selfless concern for the well-being of others is not confined to the human race. Kindness is as natural a trait to a chimp or a penguin as it is to your next-door neighbor. It's the virtual glue that holds our civilization intact.

᪥᪥᪥

You already know my story, but to refresh your memory, I will review just a few of the numerous times in my life, starting in childhood, in which I found joy and fulfillment from having made a difference in the lives of others. In some cases, it was a simple matter of charity. In others, it was about fulfilling a purpose. Often these principles overlap with meaningfulness, so I will attempt to address each issue. Please note that many of the following examples required me to be sufficiently successful in order to help finance the needs of others. But you can be sure there were far more occasions, mostly forgotten, when I extended a hand in friendship and shared the benefit of my knowledge, my advice, or simply provided reassurance and a shoulder to lean on.

When I was thirteen, I built a radio station in Eretz Israel/Palestine and taught a group of my classmates how to broadcast. This was a nascent industry in that part of the world at the time. The station became successful, and the lives of my friends, as well as my own, were positively affected. I also broke through government regulations regarding advertising when I promoted a local record store in exchange for permission to broadcast their recordings. Conclusion: I trained my friends and classmates in a useful skill and I helped set the industry for greater profitability through sponsorship. I also helped the record store increase their sales.

Two years later, I fought with the Haganah against the British. That paved the way for the War of Independence, during which time the legendary General Moshe Dayan asked me to set up a broadcasting station on Mount Scopus to facilitate communication with the army. Conclusion: In some small way, my participation helped achieve the victory that would usher in the new State of Israel.

My initial goal after college graduation in the United States was to return to Israel and help build the nascent television industry. On my first post-college job at Weston Electric in New Jersey I filed a patent on a recording device to control the temperature of up to twenty-four processes simultaneously. As a result, I made my company about $40 million a year, which, no doubt, resulted in greater job security for a number of my co-workers. Years later, my temperature control device was used by an Israeli scientist, Alexander Zarchin, in developing a desalination process using water from the Red Sea. Then, in November 1965, the lights went out in Northeastern states of the U.S. and parts of Ontario, Canada. My temperature control device was part of that electrical system. In 1986, after the nuclear accident in Chernobyl, I saw TV footage revealing the presence of my instruments in the Russian laboratories. In Israel, I also saw them connected with patients at Jerusalem's Hadassah Hospital. Before it was replaced by digital technology, my invention was used worldwide. Conclusion: Not only did my device provide me with a boost to my nascent career, but it humbled me by how, indirectly or otherwise, I made such a difference in the lives of so many.

During the 1970s, while still living in New York, I helped Danny Thomas sponsor several of his annual telethons for St. Jude's Hospital in Memphis, Tennessee. Conclusion: Helping to fund the treatment of sick children and research cures for their ills was one of the greatest undertakings of my life.

During the early1980's I helped to finance the Great Synagogue in Jerusalem, which was intended to compensate Israel for the destruction of the Second Temple of biblical times. The synagogue became an immediate success as well as the new place of worship for Prime Minister Menachem Begin. Conclusion: Being in a position to create something of value for the ages provides one of the highest levels of happiness known to man.

Over the course of the eighties, real estate did not represent the best investment. In the process of looking for a new enterprise, I became involved in the breeding of super cows for the purpose of producing a greater volume of milk for the general public. All went well until the government declared a surplus, rendering the industry barely profitable. That's when we began sending our excess to Third World countries in dire need of milk for their malnourished population. During this period, you may recall, I mentored the son of my business partners, who emerged a more mature and grounded young man Conclusion: Reinventing your own life often allows you the opportunity to reinvent the lives of others.

When I met my second wife, a young British woman, she had plans to become a dentist. I financed her dental schooling, and, although the marriage didn't last, her dental career is still flourishing. Conclusion: Sometimes the original intention of a relationship is superseded by a far different, more lasting one. Here again, I was in a position to provide the funding to make someone's dream come true.

A young woman I met a few years later showed great potential for real estate development, so I taught her the business. I did the same for her equally talented brother. As a result, within a couple of years, they both became financially independent. They are now brilliantly successful in their own enterprise. Conclusion: Helping young talent is gratifying. These siblings had personal difficulties to overcome, but with a renewed sense of purpose, they exceeded all expectations, including, perhaps, their own.

My charming and talented grandson, Jonathan, had ambitions to become a fashion designer. Neiman-Marcus has sold his collection and several major celebrities have worn his creations. But he needed funding for his earlier collections, and I was able to fill that need.

Over the course of my life, I have provided a financial lifeline to a number of people — friends, family, and sometimes virtual strangers. In nearly every case, it is not about reimbursement. What makes the giving so worthwhile for me is the joy I derive from making a difference in someone's life. Unless you can well afford such high-priced benevolence, however, sponsorship may not be an option for you. But what *is* an option for all of us — a smile, a kind word, and an ear to listen. Always remember that a small act of kindness makes someone's day, which invariably makes our own.

According to William James: "Three things in human life are important. The first is to be kind. The second is to be kind. And the third is to be kind." The Talmud addresses the issue in much the same way: "The highest wisdom is loving kindness." Anne Frank wrote: "No one has ever become poor by giving." And John Bunyan said: "You have not lived until you have done something for someone who can never repay you."

Make it a habit of repeating the giving process on a regular basis, and you have an endless stream of happiness coming your way. Some acts of giving are more difficult, longer term, and require special skills and talents. But, big or small, you have the power to change at least one life for the better. In many cases, you have already performed such acts and may not be aware of the difference you made. Think of the classic Christmas film, *It's a Wonderful Life*. James Stewart's character believes he is a failure until an angel helps him review his life and points out the many life-changing deeds he did for others.

This may come as a surprise. According to a number of studies, our definition of happiness changes as we age. The older we get, the less we equate it with excitement, and the more we define it as stability and calm. Invariably, we look less to the future for our happiness and more to the present. Another thought-provoker is that some of our greatest happiness comes in the aftermath of difficult circumstances, even crises. That we are able to survive such experiences is empowering. They challenge us to grow and to find meaning in our lives on a daily basis. I challenge you to do the same.

In case you need a few prompts to get started, I offer you this list, which is designed to trigger additional ideas of your own. If you are already doing some of these, just keep it up and take on a few new ones as you go.

Should you enjoy a good challenge, you might want to test yourself. Take two points for every one of these following items that you have previously done in your life, and see how your score compares with others.

1. Volunteer at a fundraising event.
2. Volunteer to assist in your children's classroom.
3. Volunteer at a food kitchen on Thanksgiving or another special holiday.
4. Volunteer at an animal shelter.
5. Volunteer at a senior center or home for the aging.
6. Volunteer at a local children's hospital.
7. Volunteer at a homeless shelter.

8. Volunteer at your place of worship or institution of learning.

9. Help de-litter the highway. The beach. The park. Or any public property.

10. Help a handicapped or elderly person with their shopping.

11. Help a child with homework.

12. Help make a sick child's dream come true.

13. Help a fellow driver who appears to be in distress.

14. Drive a friend or family member to and/or from a surgical appointment.

15. Drive someone to the airport, and/or pick them up.

16. Donate clothing, household items to a charity of your choice.

17. Donate gifts to an orphanage on Christmas.

18. Donate old books to your local library.

19. Donate food to a homeless shelter.

20. Take care of someone's pets and/or plants while they are away.

21. Take visitors on a tour of the city.

22. Invite a stranger to dinner.

23. Invite someone to a special event they otherwise could not afford.

24. Offer a loan to someone who may never be able to pay you back.

25. Offer to help someone de-clutter their house or clean out their garage.

26. Offer your extra bedroom to someone visiting your town.
27. Offer to babysit for a friend or family member.
28. Be an active member of a charitable foundation.
29. Be available to someone in crisis.
30. Teach someone how to do something new.
31. Teach someone tips on self-reliance.
32. Tutor a foreign-born person in English.
33. Read books to the blind, the elderly, or to sick children.
34. Record audiobooks for the blind.
35. Mentor someone in your area of expertise.
36. Remember someone's birthday.
37. Do something special for your spouse on your anniversary.
38. Listen to a friend who needs to vent or who seeks your advice.
39. Make someone feel good about themselves.
40. Walk a neighbor's dog.
41. Do something you don't enjoy just to please someone else.
42. Send a loving message to someone who would appreciate the thought.
43. Forgive someone who has wronged you.
44. Give someone a compliment.
45. Smile at strangers.
46. Show gratitude for any small favor.
47. Run an errand for a busy someone.

48. Nurse someone back to health.
49. Visit someone in the hospital.
50. Pick up a stray dog or cat and find its owner.

Over the course of your lifetime, you may have the opportunity to do something especially noble, like saving someone's life or their job or their self-respect. But in the meantime, you are fully focused on the task at hand, which is to give with your whole heart, and help make the world a better place — one situation at a time. What you are doing for the other person could be life-altering. What you are doing for yourself could be just as important or more so. Ultimately, you could be guaranteeing yourself a life of lasting happiness — particularly when you combine your purposefulness with some of the classic ingredients I discuss below.

ॐॐॐ

Happiness has been attributed to everything from a warm puppy to a winning lottery ticket to falling in love — with tens of thousands of unrelated entities and nonentities in between. None of these attributions is entirely relevant, and yet, at some point or another, every one of them is. Because for all of us seeking happiness — and that means every one of us — we see it according to our unique worldview and our current set of circumstances. Ultimately, it feels like the end result of getting everything we like, love, respect, envy, admire, and crave, all rolled into one — but all too often just one at a time, and for a limited period. So, how to rezone happiness for greater dependability, sustained satisfaction, and on a far broader scale? That's what we want to know. Right? But, is it doable? Read the rest of this chapter, and you will see that it is.

Over the centuries most great thinkers have at some point in their lives weighed in on their own recipe for happiness. Some have offered it in the form of wit, such as when Albert Einstein uncharacteristically suggested: "A table, a chair, a bowl of fruit, and a violin. What else does a man need to be happy?" George Sand, author and great love of composer Frederic Chopin, defined it more romantically. "There is only one happiness in this life, to love and be loved." The late best-selling author, Norman Cousins, never offered himself as a guru on happiness, but as an expert on laughter, which he likened to "inner jogging." He had already applied the principle to his debilitating disease when he wrote the groundbreaking bestseller, *Anatomy of an Illness*, knowing, first-hand, about the healing powers of humor. Laughter is basically good for your health because it calms the body, reduces stress, boosts your immune system, and is known to relax your muscles for the better part of an hour — making you feel exceedingly good. And since feeling good is generally synonymous with happiness — well, I rest my case. Then there was nineteenth-century Russian author Leo Tolstoy and his thoroughly pragmatic approach to happiness. He said: "If you want to be happy, *be*." Tolstoy's advice was similar in its simplicity to that of Abraham Lincoln, who is frequently credited for saying, "Man is as happy as he makes up his mind to be." And, who would dispute such logic?

Okay, then. So everyone has their own formula for happiness. And all of them work — some of the time. But you may argue that many of us have more difficult lives than others. Sure, it's easy to be happy when things are going well. But what if you are in ill health, unemployed, bankrupt, in a miserable marriage, lost your best friend — or, if possible, worse? The simple answer is, do your research and you will find what I have found (and mentioned earlier) — that some of the unhappiest people on earth are among the wealthiest, most famous, most beautiful, and most envied. If that were not true, how else to account for the overwhelming number of uber-celebrities, who, despite their good fortune, have destroyed their lives through drug addiction, serial marriages and divorces, and sometimes even suicide? Conversely, some of the happiest people on earth are the poorest, the plainest, and the most perennially put-upon. Much of the problem, then, seems to stem from expectations — unrealistic and/or unfulfilled — suggesting that most of us perceive the material world as the key to our happiness, rather than the other way around.

Material things can make you happy for a short time. We all know that. But, at least, they *do* make you happy. And what exactly is happiness for the overwhelming majority of us but short bursts of euphoria followed by long durations of deprivation?

For example — imagine you are biting into the most mouth-watering, oversized slice of oven-warm deep-dish pizza this side of Sicily or Brooklyn. A dozen delectable flavors and smells are simultaneously invading your sensory paths. Each succeeding bite takes you deeper into an exalted state of ecstasy. The grin on your face is contagious. Everyone around you aspires to the delirious exhilaration you appear to be enjoying in this exquisite moment. But time moves along at its usual pace and, before long, you have consumed the entire object of your desire and are dabbing your lips to seal your satisfaction. By now, the tantalizing tastes and smells have receded beyond recognition. The excitement has diminished to zero. The experience is history. You loved it, you ate it, it's over. Now, what? Well, I don't know, exactly — what's for dessert?

Or...

You are driving your factory-new Mercedes-Benz S-Class Sedan off the lot — the one you'd admired for weeks through the showroom window. You couldn't wait to own it so you could show it off to your friends and neighbors — a reflection of how far you've come in this dollars-and-cents world. But once you've done that, and you've successfully managed to incur the envy of your inner circle, the initial thrill is essentially gone. True, pride of ownership lasts a bit longer, but eventually that feeling is tempered, as well. After all, a car is still only a means of transportation — no matter how expensive, exclusive, and sleek. And a few months from now, its shiny replacement will emerge in the showroom — even more expensive, exclusive, and sleek. So, no — the Mercedes doesn't do it, either. Well, okay — maybe just a little.

Or...

Money. Cold, hard currency. Money buys you anything you desire, depending on how much you have in the bank. It can as easily acquire you a diamond tiara or a majestic mansion or a nuclear-powered yacht as it can deliver you great power and influence — even a coterie of fans, fair-weather friends, and ardent lovers. What's wrong with any of that, I ask? And, specifically, I ask those of you who have had your share of wealth and all it can buy, and are still running short in the happiness department. Isn't it true that money makes the world go around?

Or is it love that does it? Maybe that's it. But most of us misinterpret how love works. We expect it as an entitlement, a birthright of life on earth — as if some invisible force is charged with delivering it to us with no preconditions or term limits. If that's the kind of love you're seeking, good luck. We have all seen from experience that externally driven happiness is a sometime thing — in which case, we can only count on ourselves for its long-term existence. It's a simple formula, really: outgoing love = incoming love, but not always in equal proportion, or in perpetuity. So, if you expect love to light up your existence forever, it is up to you to screw in the bulb — and to faithfully replace it the instant it burns out.

Because the pursuit of happiness is so vital to our existence, our Founding Fathers wrote it into the Declaration of Independence as a human right. But Thomas Jefferson's words are often misquoted. He never promised the right to happiness, only the right to *pursue* it.

Motivational speaker Denis Waitley's version reads: "It is not in the pursuit of happiness that we find fulfillment, it is in the happiness of pursuit." Not long after the original was written, Guillaume Appolinaire, eighteenth-century French poet, said it this way: "Now and then it's good to pause in our pursuit of happiness and just be happy." There are other versions, as well, but they all point to the same fact. Happiness is not based on a conscious effort or expectation; it is the reward you receive along the way for living from a positive perspective.

No one denies that happiness is a state of being much to be desired. In that regard, a number of reputable studies and courses have been conducted over the years to target those elements responsible for its existence and to provide a nugget or two on how to better incorporate it into our lives. As you will notice, most formulas use similar ingredients.

According to an online article, *The Key to Happiness? It's in the Science*, by Liz Mak (March 29, 2016) the science director of the Greater Good Science Center at UC Berkeley, Emiliana Simon-Thomas, PhD, defines happiness, in part, as "being quick at recovering from negative emotions — although you do experience them — and having a sense of meaning and purpose that is tied to the collective — which, in lay terms indicates that you are contributing in a meaningful way to the people around you." (I told you so.) Her "six habits of happiness worth cultivating" are the same or variations of those expressed by her colleagues across the spectrum:

- forgiveness
- mindfulness
- gratitude
- kindness

- warm relationships
- physical fitness

Public radio station KALW's Hana Baba spoke with Dacher Keltner, author of *Born to be Good* and co-director of the Greater Good Science Center. She confirmed the following trends among the happiest of people in their studies:

- close friendships
- sharing of personal feelings for relief of stress and depression
- positive communication

The 75-year-long Harvard Study of Adult Development came to similar conclusions — that the most effective indicator of lasting happiness and well-being is the quality of our relationships with:

- family
- friends
- spouses
- associates

In a *Forbes* online article, Travis Bradberry offers *10 Habits of Incredibly Happy People*. Here is my take on these habits.

1. They slow down to appreciate life's little pleasures. This means enjoying things as simple as savoring a meal,

reveling in the aftermath of a satisfying conversation, and taking a deep breath of fresh air upon opening the front door.

2. They exercise. A mere ten minutes of movement releases GABA, the body's neurotransmitter responsible for soothing the brain and controlling your impulses.

3. They spend money on other people. Research indicates that spending money on others makes you happier than spending it on yourself. This may be the reason we take so much pleasure in holiday shopping and for birthdays and anniversaries.

4. They surround themselves with the right people. By contrast, negative people are magnets for negative circumstances, which they carry with them wherever they go. Dump them without hesitation. Exchange them for people who are worthy of your company and from whom you can learn and be inspired.

5. They stay positive. When dismissing negative people from your life, seek out the positive in your friends and associates. They will teach, support, and inspire you.

6. They get enough sleep. The connection between sleep and happiness is the sense of well-being you get following a good night of rest. Don't deprive yourself.

7. They have deep conversations. Engage with others on a deeper level than the average conversation. Discussions on meaningful topics create a closer bond of understanding among the participants.

8. They help others. Supporting others raises your own level of happiness as much as it does for the people you help. (As I was saying…)

9. They make an effort to be happy. At any given time you have a choice to either complain about something or to be happy. Regardless of your current situation, choose to be happy.

10. They have a growth mindset. Happy people embrace challenges. They see them as opportunities and a cause to take action.

Study director Dr. Robert Waldinger, Zen priest and Harvard professor of psychiatry, said in his 2016 TED talk that fostering and maintaining strong relationships helps protect against mental illness, memory decline, and chronic disease. In his article, *9 Ways to Ensure Your Relationship is Built to Last*, he specified that it isn't the number of relationships we have, but their quality and depth that matter.

So we know that strong relationships foster health and happiness, but how do we cultivate them? Waldinger's answer: "Giving people our full, undivided attention is one of the most important things we have to offer." In today's world, that means, among other nasty habits and addictions, sacrificing some of our "me time" on those assorted devices we hold dear. What that frees us to do is communicate like in the "good old days" of ten or more years ago: make eye contact with someone, listen to what they have to say, and, when appropriate, offer the benefit of our wisdom and support.

Humans still respond best to other humans who pay close attention, share their feelings, and validate their existence. This type of personal interaction registers heavily on the happiness scale — on both sides of the ledger.

Conversely, we can choose to be lonely, which, of any state of being in the universe, is the least enviable and measurably heightens personal risk to health, happiness, and well-being. How do we know? The numerous clinical and university studies, too many to mention here, unequivocally tell us so. For further details, feel free to investigate the topic all across the internet, where the case has been heavily authenticated. Keyword: "loneliness." You might also add: "ill health," since they are so closely connected. But what is to be done with those who stubbornly choose to remain diehard pessimists and/or ungrateful jerks? Numerous studies have been conducted on this topic, and the general conclusion thus far is hopeful — that is, for those ready to forego their self-absorption, and open up to the outside world.

From a nonclinical perspective, it's as clear to me as it was to Tolstoy and Lincoln — if you want to be happy, *be*. Find a way to get rid of the negativity that's holding you back, no matter how overwhelming the task. Help is out there. Don't be afraid to ask. Every day you remain in denial is another day less to enjoy. Act as though it matters to you. It should.

A few habits to practice for a life of sustained and exalted happiness:

Enjoy the moment.

This sounds easier in theory than in practice. How many hours a day do we spend waiting for someone, complaining about something, busily filling in spaces of time with wasteful thoughts or actions? We are in essence wishing away our day, hoping for a better tomorrow. What we don't take into account is that tomorrow is likely to deliver more of the same. So, in order to savor the moment in which we are living, it's essential to accept it for what it is. No matter the drudgery or distress it might represent, it is up to us to find or create something about it that is personally satisfying.

And this same exercise applies in every circumstance — even when spending an hour in a dentist's chair undergoing a root canal. Think about it. While you are sitting there, would you prefer to ruminate about the discomfort you are feeling and the high cost of the procedure — things you haven't the power to change? Or would you be better inclined to concentrate on the fact that, in a matter of moments, this procedure will be behind you and so will your toothache? Do you bother to listen, in the meantime, to the calming music filtering through the room, whose sole reason for being is to soothe and comfort you? Do you consider using this quiet time to think pleasant thoughts — like how much you admire the painting on the wall or how gracefully the trees bend with the breeze outside the window?

A perfect example of a stressful environment is what happened to me, and, I might add, to hundreds of other travelers at Los Angeles International Airport one recent Friday. Sleep-deprived in the pre-dawn morning, I arrived at the departure gate on time. The problem was that my flight did not — and the next one I could get would leave seven hours later. That was a lot of time to spend in a state of exhaustion at a terminal filled with strangers, most of them carrying on an intimate relationship with their iPhones or chasing after their restless children or snacking on some foul-smelling fast food in the seat next to mine. Then it occurred to me — this was a perfect time to practice what some experts call "mindfulness" or "living in the moment."

Mindfulness, which has its roots in Eastern philosophies like Taoism, Buddhism, and Native American spirituality, does not advocate simply putting on a happy face and ignoring the facts. Rather, it teaches you to accept "what is" in a given moment, to put it into perspective, and to go with the flow. Miraculously or not, this simple principle makes time seem to pass at record velocity. In my case, the exercise required that I end my internal dialogue about the faulty state of aviation today and the inferior quality of customer care. Instead, I became instantly grateful for one important fact: my birthday was coming up next Wednesday, the same day my driver's license was due to expire. I had brought with me the official handbook of the Department of Motor Vehicles and this delay would give me the opportunity to concentrate on studying for the computerized test. With my priorities at the fore, and my mind in the much touted flow, the next thing I knew, I had memorized all the key information, and it was time to board my midafternoon flight. P.S. I aced the test.

Mindfulness is not something to master in a day, but the more you practice, the more happiness comes your way.

Accentuate the positive.

In a June 17, 2017, *Success* article by Larry Alton, he offers *Seven Practical Steps to Achieve a Positive Mindset*. I recommend you integrative these five into your daily routine.

- Wake up each morning with expectations of positive outcomes.
- Focus on small things so as not to be overwhelmed.
- Concentrate on the present, turning negative talk to positive.
- Learn from your experiences.
- Surround yourself with optimists.

Why is it crucial to be optimistic? Well, think about it. Have you ever met a happy pessimist? Malcontents, cynics, and misanthropes thrive on disaster and disappointment. If only good news were to greet them, they might be forced to rezone their thinking — and that could ruin their entire day.

Twentieth-century concert pianist/author/actor/comedian Oscar Levant found humor in his trademark despair, which for negative thinkers and neurotics is their preferred state of being. One of his classic quips bears witness to his state of mind:

"I was once thrown out of a mental hospital for depressing the other patients." Another favorite: "Schizophrenia beats dining alone." On happiness, he was more profound and bordering on the optimistic: "Happiness isn't something you experience, it's something you remember."

Of the estimated 12,000 to 60,000 thoughts we humans process on a daily basis, 80 percent of them are known to be negative. That means we think negatively 8,000 to 48,000 separate times during a 24-hour cycle. I am not advocating for an uninterrupted stream of happy thoughts all day long. Sometimes we need to think negatively — such as when taking precautions crossing a street in heavy traffic or confronting a hostile stranger in a dark alley. Negative thoughts help keep us alert and protect our safety under precarious circumstances. But the fact that they occupy so much of our day makes them all the more difficult to contain. That's why a little levity, as Oscar Levant practiced, helps neutralize the gravity.

Filmmaker/actor/comedian/musician Woody Allen is our contemporary master of neurotic humor. He is successful, in part, because he makes us look at our own bag of troubles and realize we're all in this together. In particular, Woody Allen is famous for fearing death and making his audience see the inherent humor in all things negative. For example, he is well known for saying, "Life is full of misery, loneliness, and suffering — and it's all over much too soon." There is also his classic: "I'm not afraid of dying. I just don't want to be there when it happens." In these two statements, he has verbalized one of humankind's greatest fears, and rendered it — temporarily, at least — benign. To demonstrate the futility of trying to convert a negative thinker to positive, I offer Allen's clever but intentionally convoluted commentary on love and happiness: "To avoid suffering one must not love. But then one suffers from not loving. Therefore, to love is to suffer; not to love is to suffer; to suffer is to suffer. To be happy is to love. To be happy, then, is to suffer, but suffering makes one unhappy. Therefore, to be happy one must love or love to suffer or suffer from too much happiness." I warned you it was convoluted.

A lot of our negative thinking is generated from taking ourselves too seriously or worrying about things that likely will never come to pass. While it would be futile for even the most optimistic of us to pursue a negative-free existence, diminishing some of our darkest thoughts with humor can go a long way toward shedding the light.

Have something to look forward to.

Whoever invented the concept of vacation had happiness in mind — giving us, besides the experience, something to look forward to as well as look back upon. It's all about taking a break from routine. By contrast, consider a variation on Einstein's formula for insanity: doing the same thing over and over again without a change of pace.

Twilight Zone was a classic sci-fi TV series of the 1960s. Of the 150+ episodes aired, one illustrated this concept as profoundly as anything I've seen. The unsympathetic central character was given to a life of excess — that meant partying around the clock and overdosing on women, booze, and, in general, *la dolce vita*. Eventually the Devil caught up with him and sent him to Hell. What did Hades look like to our dead, departed party-boy? The same fast and furious lifestyle he was living on earth — but this time, he would be doing it nonstop, fast forward, and for the rest of eternity. Here again we have a case of "too much of a good thing" — this time, on steroids.

Taking a break from your routine doesn't necessitate a two-week vacation. In fact, the most effective break I can think of for reducing stress and elevating our endorphins is a daily dose of simple pleasure. I recommend spending a few minutes out of doors — rain or shine — and breathing in the offerings of Mother Nature, even if they come in the form of city smells and traffic noise. Take a walk, sniff the flowers, watch a squirrel run across the street, stop to talk to a dog on a leash as well as the human on the other end. Occasionally, plan a drive outside of town to enjoy lunch or dinner in the countryside. Sense those endorphins multiplying throughout your bloodstream by the simple act of mingling with the world outside of your comfort zone. It makes the time spent doing the most mundane of life's chores a lot more tolerable — even appealing. For example: have you ever noticed how much you wanted to get away and then how equally happy you were to be back home?

Lead a balanced existence.

Is it possible to balance the various segments of our lives — family, social, health, career, financial, civic, and spiritual? Probably not. The goal here is not to achieve perfect balance, but to avoid spending an 80-hour week at our workplace and zero quality time with loved ones, including ourselves. Balance requires paying attention to the needs of those around us, while not ignoring our own. The greater the external balance we achieve, the greater sense of well-being we generate within. And we already know that happiness and well-being are intimately related.

Nurture your relationships — love and otherwise. These are the key to your survival.

You may be deluded into believing you are in constant communication with friends and loved ones — courtesy of Facebook, Twitter, Instagram, and text-messaging. But, depending on your generation, you are possibly ignorant of what it was like not long ago when, in order to keep in touch with people, "touch" was the operative word. As recently as 2005, it would not have been socially acceptable to sit across a dinner table from someone you love, and, rather than engage them in conversation with a touch of the hand, choose, instead, to respond to an electronic message inside a small rectangular box. Is intimacy dead or has it merely become "device-ive"?

Of all the primary criteria for happiness, this is one on which there is total unanimity among the experts. People need people. And those who have them are the "luckiest people in the world." My message to you is, never take your "people" for granted. Treat them as though they are precious to you. If you don't, chances are someone else will. The options online these days count in the billions, and *you* count only as one. The beauty of the process online is that it is so easy to implement.

All you have to do is smile at someone and say hello. How hard is that, when you consider that this one gesture could mean a lifelong friendship and an ongoing support system?

Some people are famous for being famous and wealthy — and others are famous for *marrying* the famous and wealthy. The woman to whom I now refer belongs in the latter category. She has been married more than once, and each time to someone of prominence, great wealth, and/or political influence. During an interview she gave some years back, she was asked how she had managed to make some of the most eligible (and even not-so-eligible) men on the planet fall in love with her. Her frank answer was that when she was with a man, even in a crowd, she focused on him as though he were the only person in the world. Granted, this was before social media stepped in to distract us. But still — the human instinct remains the same. People tend to gravitate to people who seem to gravitate to them. In the case of the woman in question, she initially netted her last husband's attention at a lavish banquet, when she spontaneously tossed him a dinner roll over the heads of a few distinguished guests. He immediately caught on to her intentions as well as the roll, and the rest, as they say, is well documented. This woman's story is a wake-up call to those of us less spontaneous or free-spirited — in the hope it serves as inspiration.

So, even though the delivery of our human-to-human messaging has changed in recent times, the nature of our species has not — nor have our personal needs. Relationships are vital to our sense of well-being and even our purpose in life. For the good of your health and longevity, as well as your peace of mind, your job is to develop solid new relationships, preserve and even improve upon those that already work for you, and, dispose of those that fail to make the grade. Like cigarettes and other toxic substances, the wrong relationships may pose a serious hazard to your health. That is no exaggeration. Just ask your trusted physician.

In matters of endorphin-producing love, however, always offer the benefit of the doubt. Give and return it with equal enthusiasm.

Show gratitude.

You are alive and reading these words. That, alone, gives you reason to be grateful every day of the week. Anything more than that is a bonus, and requires a lot more attention. Whether you are sitting home alone, or out in public, there are multitudes of ways in which to show gratitude and far more reasons for doing so.

Why is gratitude so important a prerequisite to happiness? For one thing, it allows you to inventory the things in your life that deserve recognition for the value they add to your existence. For another, it encourages you to reach out and validate those around you. How good does it feel to praise, let's say, a customer service representative at your cable company for helping reconnect your service after a breakdown? Yes, these people are paid for helping you. But you get paid, too, for thanking them. Remember: not everything worth appreciating returns a dollar equivalent.

Never underestimate the power of prayer as a primary means of giving thanks, as it often provides rewards as nothing else. But personal gratitude — incoming and outgoing — also benefits your state of well-being. Take notice of those seemingly incidental times throughout the day when you have the opportunity to be appreciative. Play a little game with yourself by counting the times you choose to express your appreciation, whether passively or actively. How incredibly good, after a long day of doing that, does it make you feel? Yes, I thought so. Repeat the process tomorrow. Eventually it will become a habit that predictably results in radiant inner joy. It doesn't get any better than that.

Be altruistic.

Giving to others and acts of kindness are part of a vital mindset, which I discussed earlier in greater detail, but is more than worth repeating.

Follow your passion. Do the work you love and love the work you do.

Some of us cannot avoid the need to work a 9-to-5 existence at a humdrum job just to pay the rent. So following your passion may be a luxury you think you can't afford. If this describes you, do not dismiss your dreams too lightly. There are ways to make it happen. The first and most important step is to isolate your passion and create an action plan. Maybe you work in a bank during the day, have three kids and a spouse at home, and help your resistant eight-year-old with his math homework every night. Time-consuming, no doubt, and exhausting. But, if you set out to redirect some of your leisure time — even just a couple of nights or early mornings a week — you have the bare beginnings of a new life schedule that includes, even highlights, the path to your dreams.

But sometimes a dream is never meant to be more than that — a dream. I knew a man some years ago, an engineer, who considered himself a deep thinker, and fancied the notion of becoming a published author. The only problem was, he had a wife and three children to support. Eventually, he and his wife inherited a great deal of money, which made him financially independent — and perfectly poised to pursue any path of his choice. But more years passed him by. His children were grown, he went into retirement, and had more time than ever to practice his passion. But, did he? No. Even though he may not have realized, that was his goal all along — the unrealized dream. And that is how too many of us spend our lives — wishing we could do something and then making excuses why we can't. Ultimately, inaction leaves an empty space in our minds, where happiness and fulfillment have been permanently short-changed. Yet, for some of us needing an ongoing excuse for discontentment, this one effectively serves the purpose.

But there is more to following your passion than the steps I have begun to outline. In fact, there are those who express a technical disagreement with my advice. Cal Newport, a computer science professor at Georgetown University and author of *So Good They Can't Ignore You,* contends that "American culture is obsessed with the idea that we need to 'find our passion' in order to be happy and successful" and that "passion is not a preexisting condition" but the end-product of our efforts. According to Newport, we develop passion only by "consciously building a unique talent and then using it to take control of our career path." As long as we become so good at what we do and work hard at doing it, the world will take notice and honor us accordingly. Being honored for something we do well not only sparks our passion, but, more often than not, it makes us happy.

Newport was inspired by Steve Jobs, who told an audience of students in 2005 that if they hadn't yet found their passion to keep looking, and to not settle for anything less. Jobs was speaking from his own experience. He had not set out to create the groundbreaking smart phone technology he eventually did — along with the help of geniuses like Steve Wozniak. He fell upon it in the course of doing business and honing his craft. So, while it is advantageous to be born with a strong affinity and seemingly innate talent like Mozart, it is more the anomaly than the rule.

As Newport described the process that carried Steve Jobs to the pinnacle of success, "he built up a rare and valuable skill and then used that skill as leverage to take control of his working life and shift it in the direction that most resonated with him." The bottom line is that you cannot expect a really rewarding working life unless you are particularly good at something. And you become really good at it by doing it repeatedly and often. In his bestselling *Outliers*, Malcolm Gladwell made an excellent case for 10,000 hours of experience on any given task or topic as the magic number that transports you from amateur to expert. So much for "overnight success."

And for those of you who have found yourself becoming a heart surgeon or an insurance agent despite your love for the saxophone, be assured you aren't alone. I know an entertainment attorney who leads a full and happy life doing what he does, and that is due in large part to finding an outlet for his music — an orchestra made up entirely of like-minded attorneys. This is also valid advice for those who are pressured into working the family business or fulfilling a parent's dream rather than their own. If extricating yourself is out of the question, you can still fulfill your desires by dedicating a separate niche to it in your daily life. Who knows? One day that separate niche might become strong enough to allow you to hand over the business to more interested family members and to rezone yourself on the path you have long aspired to follow.

Whether you think you have a passion for something or not, you can find it — or even develop it — by loving what you do. Either way, life is enjoyed all the more when you treasure each moment, however unremarkable. It's the unremarkable moments, after all, where we spend most of our lives.

Now you know what you're really after, don't you? A higher level of happiness than you have enjoyed in the past. And it's been waiting for you all along. It's waiting for you right now. But you know better than to expect it to come to you. It's *you* who has to pursue *it*. However, you must be enlightened and appreciative enough to recognize its illusory nature and be willing to work — not only to achieve it, but, more importantly, to sustain and preserve it. It's a proactive process that never ends. As Buddha said, *No one saves us but ourselves. No one can and no one may. We ourselves must walk the path.*

If this chapter has even begun to help you rezone to a loftier level — well, to borrow the classic phrase of legendary entertainer Al Jolson, *You ain't seen nothin' yet.*

છે છે છે

Three essentials to happiness in life are something to do, something to love, and something to hope for.

~ Joseph Addison

છે છે છે

CHAPTER 20

REZONE FOR HAPPINESS: PART II

HAPPINESS equals REALITY minus EXPECTATIONS

~ Manel Baucells and Rakesh Sarin

೪೪೪

Because you cannot have too much happiness, and because I am an engineer at heart, I am herewith presenting a bonus chapter on happiness. This one is inspired by *Engineering Happiness: A New Approach for Building a Joyful Life* by Manel Baucells and Rakesh Sarin (University of California Press, 2012). As professional engineers, the authors were inspired to formulate "the fundamental equation of happiness" within a series of six laws or principles that govern our emotions. According to Baucells and Sarin, through the "planning and acting on [of] these six principles, happiness becomes a controllable and predictable possibility." Just keep in mind that happiness means different things to different people, albeit with one common determinant — expectations. Without the demands of expectations in either direction — high or low — it is impossible to be disappointed. And where disappointment is absent or, at least, limited in scope, satisfaction and pleasure have an easier time of filling the gap.

Baucells and Sarin assure their readers that happiness is a choice. So, based on their approach, they agree with Abraham

Lincoln and his oft-quoted contention that man really *is* as happy as he makes up his mind to be. They advise their readers as follows:

> Carefully examine your life and determine which factors are important to you. Most people want a job they enjoy, financial security, good health, and fulfilling relationships. But you must be proactive in moving toward the goals that are important to you. Eat right and exercise is not just a slogan if you want good health in the long run. You must come up with a plan for a healthier lifestyle, make choices consistent with your plan, and monitor your progress. With effort and determination, eating right and exercise will become a habit and you will be on the road to a healthier life. A similar game plan can be devised to achieve the ultimate objective: happiness.

To that end, they identified "thirteen pillars of happiness" that, with practice, would help you build a better life. Basically, they focus on the way you eat, sleep, work, love, socialize, and how you perceive the quality of your life as you take on these basic aspects of life. The primary rule is to implement the best possible strategy in each instance, and repeat it until it becomes a habit, thereby creating new neural pathways and reinforcing it as second nature. By seeking out and adapting the most satisfying ways of performing routine actions, you are proactively improving the quality of your daily existence — making it vastly more pleasurable, and even healthier and more functional. So, if it sounds more like a case of deliberate planning and less like a spontaneous offering, you've got the idea.

Happiness, as I previously stated, is hard work, but worth the effort. And the greater happiness you seek, the harder and more dedicated must be the work to achieve and sustain it. And, yes, to appreciate it every day of your life.

Happiness Destroyers to Avoid:

Envy. There is no one thing more fatal to your pursuit of happiness than to covet that which belongs to someone else. For instance, let's say a hard-working friend of yours is taking her vacation this year in South America. She will celebrate the Mardi Gras in Rio, dance the tango in Buenos Aires, and climb to the legendary Machu Picchu in Peru. Why does she get to go, and not you? Not fair. Learning of her good news not only ruins your day, but those negative feelings haunt you for the entire time she is gone, and beyond. Do yourself a favor and take a reality check. Ask yourself, does it make you any happier to wish yourself in her place and deprive her of the trip she worked for all year long? If the answer here is anything but no, you are much further away from achieving happiness than you might have imagined.

Taken to another level, envy can easily slip into greed and avarice, even gluttony. And if envy does not drive you to worker harder to achieve your goals rather than to wish them away from others, that's where laziness comes into play. Some of us know it as sloth. If this is beginning to sound like a laundry list of the seven deadly sins, that's the point.

How to conquer envy? Simple. Learn to appreciate what you have rather than what belongs to someone else. It is likely you possess a great number of things that others would appreciate calling their own. And if there is something you want that you don't currently have, do the work to achieve it. Not only would your efforts give you a fair shot at success, but also the satisfaction of accomplishment.

Pride. In one respect, pride is a positive trait. Taking pride in your work, for example, generally means you have achieved a goal and are satisfied with the outcome. Conversely, pride can be construed as arrogance, boasting, and bluster, and a weakness for pumping yourself up while simultaneously tearing others down.

How to overcome the negative aspect of pride? Show appreciation for the achievements and personal traits of those around you. And express gratitude for the generosity of others, as well as for the simple beauties of the world in which you live.

Anger. Expressing your displeasure with external forces by raising your voice or your fist is never a shortcut to happiness. Not only does it alienate those around you, but it ultimately reverts to the sender — yourself — which is where it belonged in the first place. Maybe you have noticed that uncontrollable anger with the outside world is generally the result of unacknowledged frustration with oneself. Something to consider working on as you set forth on your journey to cheerier shores.

So, if you want to be happy, be. But know that it takes time and commitment to get there, and to remain firmly in place. Begin by reviewing all pertinent elements of your life as they exist in today's real world and then envision how you would alter them for maximum gratification. Remind yourself that in exchange for a little discomfort now as you adjust to a new set of rules, you are on your way to experiencing a more heightened state of joy.

As you move forward, keep your optimism high and your expectations low. And know that, for good or bad, the measure of your success will most likely equal the measure of your commitment.

෩෩෩

Happiness lies in the joy of achievement and the thrill of creative effort.

~ Franklin D. Roosevelt

෩෩෩

CHAPTER 21

REZONING THE HUMAN RACE

(Adapted from Chapter 28, *Evolution by God*)

I hold that while man exists, it is his duty to improve not only his own condition, but to assist in ameliorating mankind.

~ Abraham Lincoln

ᡒᡒᡒ

And, on a lighter note...

We are all here on earth to help others;
what on earth the others are here for I don't know.

~ W. H. Auden

ᡒᡒᡒ

Descended from several generations of Talmud scholars, I have always sought to live by its principles of *Tikkun Olam*. For me, repairing the world is a lifelong passion that I hope I practice well enough to have changed a few lives for the better — if not quite the whole world. I wrote about this crucial topic in Chapter 28 of my previously published *Evolution by God*, but I felt it important enough to discuss again in this context.

Through whichever lens you are looking, and from whosever perspective across the globe, the problems of our civilization appear pretty much the same. So, too, the solutions. Below, I break them down into three general categories. As you review each one of them, remember this: it is our goal as the current prototype for the human race to unify and take transformative action. The Doomsday Clock is ticking, and if you listen you can hear it calling us to take up the challenge — which is to unify our species toward this singular goal. Repair the world. Redeem humanity. *Tikkun Olam.*

So, here's the plan:

1. **Feed the World** — Objective: the total elimination of global starvation through the development of agricultural projects and systems designed to produce massive amounts of food — as well as educational programs to teach underdeveloped nations to create a sustainable food program for their population. While the United Nations' Food and Agricultural Organization (FAO) claims that 925 million of the earth's population is currently mal- or undernourished (mostly in Asia and the Pacific, followed by Sub-Saharan Africa, Europe, and North and South America), the FAO also advises there is a sufficient worldwide food supply to keep all 6.8 billion of us from going to bed hungry at night. One has to wonder where the system breaks down to account for such staggering mismanagement, and why this issue isn't being fully investigated and resolved.

    Our first step with Feed the World would be to set up a private international nonprofit foundation to educate and enlighten representatives from other developed nations to join in the effort. As we define and refine our programs, we would be promoting them in areas desperate for the training and for the crops from which their populations would benefit. Overall, agriculture is the quickest and most efficient way to produce massive numbers of jobs. With a Feed the World program, we could train millions of workers to perform specialized functions in each phase of the operation. Primarily, we could recruit these individuals from the rolls of recent college graduates as well as retirees and the un- and underemployed. As a result, unemployment numbers across the globe would drop like stones and motivation and purpose would rise proportionately.

Just as the Jewish National Fund is dedicated to making the world a better place through agricultural innovation, renewable energy, and medical research, the Feed the World program would not be funded exclusively by mega-corporations, but by individual donations of pennies, dimes, and dollars. That means the program would essentially be inspired by a religious consciousness of tithing, practiced and reinforced with the intellectual know-how of twenty-first century science. As a child in Israel, I engaged in the daily practice of *tzedakah* by depositing my small change into the charity box on my teacher's desk. After eight years of performing such a childhood ritual as this, charity becomes a lifelong habit that passes down through the generations. In the case of Feed the World, it would expand the tradition worldwide.

Effectively operated, Feed the World would cultivate vast areas of the United States, reclaiming arid desert land for agriculture. With access to advanced technology, I believe we could achieve our goal in a relatively short period of time. Considering that America and its San Joaquin Valley in California was known not long ago as "the breadbasket of the world," it would be natural for us to make a dramatic comeback in this manner — exporting 50 percent of our crops to other countries, which would pay for the program's costs, and then donating the remaining 50 percent to needy nations, which we would simultaneously train to become agriculturally independent.

About twenty years ago, I read in *National Geographic* that the deserts of the world are continually expanding, with the notable exception of the land of Israel. As I mentioned in an earlier chapter, this phenomenon is based on the fact that Israel is continuously converting its arid land to fertile soil for agricultural use. Our plan would make this technology possible in every participating country across the globe.

We would also consider advocating for a voluntary worldwide reduction in population growth, particularly in developing nations. China implemented a similar program in the past — a move that may be largely responsible for the country's significant economic growth over these past two decades and its healthy projections into the future. By stabilizing world population, we could better maintain economic viability throughout. This would not be imposed by government mandate, but by education and birth control methods on an individual level. By 2050, the world population, currently at a bit more than 6 billion people, is expected to increase by 3.6 billion, about 60 percent of which would occur in Asia. Formerly known as The Optimum Population Trust, Population Matters has been campaigning for years to reduce projected population growth for the UK, as well as internationally. So far, the numbers are promising. Annual growth rate for 2017 was estimated at 1.11 percent (down from 1.13 percent in 2016), which still adds up to a sizeable increase of 80 million per year. As a means of saving the planet for humanity, the distinguished University of Texas ecologist Eric Pianka announced at a meeting of the Texas Academy of Science that 90 percent of the human population would have to die. His chosen means for accomplishing this would be an airborne Ebola. On a more rational level, if we are to remedy the problem humanely, it would have to be done incrementally and as a preventive measure only.

2. **Heal the World** — Objective: the gradual elimination of all diseases by way of expanded scientific research, using state-of-the-art technology and surgical tools

and techniques, as well as the latest breakthroughs in stem cell research and genetic engineering.

Through continued exploration into the workings of the brain (although at vast potential risk to our freedoms of thought and emotion), science may one day be able to engineer hatred, fear, and intolerance from the human mind. Furthermore, we could import researchers, scientists, and physicians from across the globe to join our medical community. Their common goal would be to discover cures for the deadliest and most stubborn of human and animal diseases, as well as to perform research into space exploration and the contentious issue of climate control.

In the interim, the development of early-warning devices and reinforcement of buildings would protect the world population from impending natural and man-made disasters. Also, sections of our reclaimed deserts would be made habitable in order to move populations away from potentially dangerous areas and toward safer and more hospitable havens.

By setting up an international program with foreign students and experts in their respective fields, we would prepare them to return to their countries of origin, where they would continue to work toward the program's objectives, ultimately promoting a healthier planet.

3. **Free the World of Negativity** — Objective: the development of super-smart computer technology

designed to make decisions consistently resulting in best or optimum outcomes — free of emotional bias or human error. Research and development of effective techniques could eliminate the impact of negative emotions on the same frontier as it might be conquered through medical research. (For advisory, see: #2 above, Heal the World.) Along with medical research and engineering of the human brain that could eliminate negative emotions from our DNA, we would be able to purge the human race as well as the planet of deadly disharmony. But, not so fast. We know from the movies, as well as from real life, that from within the realm of peace and harmony too often emerges a disruptive, even destructive, faction with a dark agenda of its own. So, vigilant oversight would be required by a body of neutral experts — difficult as it may seem these days to encounter human impartiality.

Think Globally, Act Massively

The good news on this front is that major philanthropists like Bill and Melinda Gates, through their Bill and Melinda Gates Foundation, are already working to eradicate global poverty and starvation, as well as certain diseases, like malaria and HIV/AIDS. The movement is duly inspired by the optimistic statistics that indicate the non-poor world population is rising while the extremely poor population is decreasing. In fact, it was three times lower in 2015 with an estimated 705 million

than it was at its peak in 1970 with 2.2 billion. This is attributable in large part to improved nutrition and more widespread
use of vaccinations.

Gates believes that "every life is valuable. That we can make
things better. That innovation is the key to a bright future.
That we're just getting started." Through their foundation, the
Gateses have been investing in what they call catalytic philanthropy — areas of our society that are being underfunded or
largely overlooked. Education is one of the top priorities on
their list for rezoning, and pandemics and poverty are among
those scourges they plan to wipe out. Since technology is where
Gates made his initial impact on society, it is understandable
that he looks to its potential for "unlocking the innate compassion we have for our fellow human beings. In the end, that
combination — the advances of science together with our
emerging global conscience — may be the most powerful tool
we have for improving the world." Says fellow innovator and
Oracle co-founder Larry Ellison, "It's Microsoft versus mankind, with Microsoft having only a slight lead." Judging from
the Gateses' dedication to improving the world, Microsoft
will be among those most responsible for helping to rezone
humankind to its full potential.

Think Specifically, Act Individually

On Martha Stewart's blog, courtesy of Clinton Global Ini-
tiative, she lists fifty-two ways to improve the world, which
breaks down into four categories: Energy and Climate Change,
Global Health, Poverty Alleviation, and Education.

She also suggests certain positive changes to our habits and lifestyles, such as:

- sharing rides
- using energy-saving utilities and fuel-efficient vehicles
- stopping smoking
- donating leftover bulk food to a homeless shelter
- teaching children about health and nutrition
- starting a mentor program in your workplace
- offering pro-bono services based on your skill sets

Charity is not only about giving money, but also your time, your talents, and yourself.

Like any other habit, charity takes a little discipline at first while you work it into your daily life. Eventually, as it becomes second nature, it takes over an essential part of your existence and you begin to see that the more you give of yourself, the significantly more you get in return. It's always amazing to realize how enormous anything is capable of becoming from even the most modest beginnings — and, as it grows stronger, how much energy it generates along the way. Every one of us has the potential to make a difference — at any age and with any level of funding or talent. It can also start with your piggy bank or that *tzedakah* box on your teacher's desk.

With all the problems facing this planet and its people today, it is overwhelming to consider the countless possibilities of what one individual can do to make the greatest impact. Surely there is some specific issue or injustice that frazzles your nerves or brings you to tears or infuriates you like nothing else. Whatever that is, it's a good place to focus, to pull out your repair kit and to start tinkering. The fact that we are all different varieties of humans — each of us with our unique quirks and qualities — means that with every challenge facing humanity, there is at least one of us out there up to the task: to meet it head-on and rezone it. And that includes you and me.

As some wise someone once said, *What is the point of being alive if you don't at least try to do something remarkable?* Humans thrive on purpose. And as long as we have that driving force blazing within us, we are capable of changing the world for the infinitely better.

ৰ্ৰ্ৰ

How wonderful it is that nobody need wait a single moment before starting to improve the world.

~ Anne Frank

ৰ্ৰ্ৰ

CHAPTER 22

PAUL, THE WORLD'S GREATEST REZONER: REZONING JUDAISM TO CHRISTIANITY

So I say to you, ask, and it will be given to you; search, and you will find; knock, and the door will be opened for you.

~ Jesus Christ

ৡৡৡ

Perhaps the greatest rezoning in the history of mankind was that of the Jewish religion — a segment of it, that is — to an offshoot upstart religion that became known as Christianity. This momentous event took place about 2,000 years ago, in large part due to the unlikely conversion of a contentious young rabbi named Saul, later and forever to be known as the Apostle Paul. Born around 4 B.C. of Roman Jewish parents of the tribe of Benjamin, Saul began life in the unremarkable town of Tarsus, located in the eastern part of modern day Turkey.

While he was still a child, Saul's family moved 350 miles to Jerusalem, where he was educated in the Torah at a strict Pharisaic rabbinical school. Grown furious with the followers of Christ for forsaking Judaism, the zealous Saul accepted the authority to arrest anyone attempting to evangelize among the Jewish community. And that is why he was on the road to Damascus that auspicious day — to seek out worshippers of Jesus and return them to Jerusalem to face trial and inevitable punishment.

As he approached the city on horseback, according to the New Testament (Acts 9:3-4), Saul was surprised by a burst of light so strong that it blinded him and caused him to fall from his horse. He was then greeted by the voice of Jesus asking why he was persecuting the Church. Led blindly on to Damascus, Saul became repentant, healed of his affliction, and was baptized accordingly.

Once the converted Paul began preaching his new gospel in Damascus, he gained a reputation as an agitator and leader of a dangerous religious sect. He is said to have escaped his detractors with the help of a few fellow Christians, who lowered him in a basket over the walls of the city, allowing him to travel back to Jerusalem. There he spent time with the Apostle Peter and became more entrenched in his faith. But word had preceded the young rabbi to the Holy City, where the Christian population was uncertain about trusting him in his newly adopted ministry.

Christianity, According to Paul

His conversion in Damascus notwithstanding, Paul called himself a "Jew of Jews," and, in his mind and heart, he remained a Jew. Like most of the early followers, Paul saw the teachings of Jesus as an extension of his Judaism — as a renewed form of the religion, not its abandonment. This positive approach to the religion was met with an equal measure of acceptance. However, when put to the test, the two religious philosophies did not completely mesh. Most significantly, they disagreed on the most basic of all their tenets. According to Judaism, people are ultimately judged according to their deeds here on Earth — the good and the bad. That's how, traditionally, any Jew would qualify for a place in "The World to Come," otherwise known as Heaven. Christian thinking, by contrast, teaches that faith in Christ, alone, is the one and only path to eternal salvation and everlasting life. And that was the most powerful device in Paul's conversion toolkit. Anyone, regardless of faith, social stature, or even immoral behavior, would be guaranteed eternal life as long as they accepted Jesus as their Lord and Savior, who, he would remind them, had died on the cross for their sins. And, for those among the wavering or skeptical, he gave assurances they could choose in His favor — even up to the moment of their death. In some instances, even now, in this twenty-first century, Mormonism extends that service even beyond death. How easy this is, then — a special place in Heaven, regardless of your deeds on Earth, in exchange for accepting Jesus as your means of getting there. Is it any wonder that Paul's ministry was spreading further across the miles with every trip he made, every letter he wrote?

Paul is quoted in Romans 10.9 as follows: "If you confess with your mouth Jesus as Lord and believe in your heart that God raised Him from the dead, you will be saved."

Paul's Marketing Plan for Rezoning Judaism

Fourteen of the twenty-seven books in the New Testament are attributed to Paul, all of which take the form of letters, generally of self-introduction, either to an individual or a religious community. The theme of these letters was to advocate for the Gospel within a world that still worshipped idols and broke Jewish laws — to address common issues, not to create an historical record. For all those non-believers, baptism was the answer. It would absolve an individual of his sins and provide him with a fresh start. Paul did not discount God's original covenant with the Jews, and assured them that by accepting Jesus as their Savior, God's promise to them would be kept. It is essential to keep in mind that these early Christians fully anticipated the Second Coming, so the element of urgency was crucial.

The period during which Paul wrote his letters was difficult for him and the growing Church, as Christianity was still little more than a series of separate communities, located great distances apart, and with no central governing body. It was also a time of severe persecution, which was clearly illustrated at the Coliseum in Rome, where, along with a hungry lion or two, Christians provided the day's entertainment to a polytheistic populace in search of a good time.

At the Council of Jerusalem in the year 49 AD, Paul argued successfully against the widespread belief that non-Jews seeking salvation would first have to convert to Judaism. Essentially, as any good sales representative would do in the interest of closing a deal, Paul satisfied their every objection: no 613 principles of Mosaic law, no circumcision, and no dietary rules. No inconveniences of any sort. They could still enjoy roast suckling pig for dinner and male newborns could still hold onto their foreskins. Such a deal! Who could resist? Who, after all, didn't want an ironclad guarantee of a spot in the Hereafter, where they could hang out with their dear departed and bask forever in the hallowed presence of the greatest force in the universe? The way Paul persuaded them, they had nothing to lose and eternity to gain.

What about evidence? No problem there. No evidence necessary. No questions necessary, either. Faith covered everything. Faith was what it was all about.

Somewhere along the way, something happened to Paul's popular brand of Judaism. It was no longer Judaism.

Judaism Light = Early Christianity

Based on existing evidence, Jesus lived and died a Jew, with no known intention of starting a new faith — merely fixing the one that he already followed. But there were those who instantly accepted him as their long-awaited Messiah, which traditional Jews did not — and therein lay the beginning of a new religious order. Expert persuader that he was, Paul was able to tune in to the masses and promise them whatever they wanted. He was now promoting the rival team that he had created inadvertently into greater prominence than his own.

Over the decades that followed, Paul was frequently in trouble with local authorities as well as local congregations of Jews and others, but he and his ministry continued to flourish.

Despite the hostility he faced in and out of prison — where he wrote a number of his most important letters — he survived and thrived for a long time to come, preaching personal salvation in the name of Jesus and accumulating vast numbers of disciples as well as building credibility for Christ. Eventually, however, Paul's outspoken defiance caught up with him one last time and he was taken to Rome as a prisoner. Although the account of his death is not described in the New Testament, it is generally believed he was convicted for his controversial teachings and summarily beheaded in Rome. His execution is said to have taken place at some time following the Great Fire in 64 — which had been blamed on the Christians — but before the end of Nero's notorious reign. It was because he was a Roman citizen that Paul was spared the agony of crucifixion and, instead, was merely beheaded for his perceived crimes. Not having enjoyed the perks of Roman citizenship, Peter, it is speculated, did not get off that easily.

During his six decades on this planet, Paul had managed to rezone his own religion into one that multiplied and flourished for thousands of miles around the civilized ancient world. And he did it by applying the salesman's timeless primary principle — fill a human need and then over-deliver.

But that was two millennia ago. How do things stack up in today's far different society? Let's examine the three major religions, all of which were inspired by the God of Abraham. The first and oldest, Judaism, now counts nearly 14.5 million followers worldwide, taking into account such population reducers as the Spanish Inquisition and the Nazi Holocaust and, yes, Christian conversion. Its two offspring religions, Christianity and Islam, boast approximately 2.5 billion and 1.5 billion, respectively. While Paul cannot be given credit for the founding of Islam, Christianity is indeed indebted to his skills of persuasion and that life-altering experience he had on the road to Damascus.

ৰ্জৰ্জৰ্জ

Summing Up

In the end, it matters little how Paul lived and died. But he should be remembered as the greatest communicator of his time — maybe of *all* time. Without benefit of anything approaching the reach of the internet, social media, TV, or radio, Paul managed to spread his ministry from its original ragtag remnant to the largest theological belief system in the world. Now that is a case of rezoning for the ages — no doubt, for eternity.

ৰ্জৰ্জৰ্জ

Owe no man anything, but to love one another: for he that loveth another hath fulfilled the law. For this, Thou shalt not commit adultery, Thou shalt not kill, Thou shalt not steal, Thou shalt not bear false witness, Thou shalt not covet; and if there be any other commandment, it is briefly comprehended in this saying, namely, Thou shalt love thy neighbor as thyself.

~ Paul, the Apostle

ৰ্জৰ্জৰ্জ

CHAPTER 23

REZONING PEOPLE:
THE REWARDING ACT OF MENTORSHIP

The delicate balance of mentoring someone is not creating them in your own image, but giving them the opportunity to create themselves.

~ Steven Spielberg

తతతత

Over the course of my lifetime, I have had a natural inclination toward sharing my knowledge with others of lesser experience, and, in most cases, with successful, even phenomenal, results. As you know by now, one of my first, unofficial, mentorships took place during childhood when I shared the nitty-gritty of running my home-based radio station with a small group of friends, who became an essential part of my production and broadcasting team. Mentorship must run in my DNA, since my grandfather taught me about business principles and ethics and also about following my heart. Knowing my interest in science, he set up a lab in his store for me so I could work there every day after school. Later on, my father, primarily a businessman who also invested in real estate, gave me practical advice as I began making my career shift away from engineering. Once I established myself in Upstate New York real estate,

I was fortunate to have a smart and honorable mentor in Charlie Patrick, whose name I had stumbled upon in a Poughkeepsie phone book. Charlie taught me a great deal about real estate investing and set me on a professional path for which I will always be grateful. In turn, I brought in a young rabbi, Sidney, as my assistant and mentee and eventually took him on as a business partner for several lucrative projects. Sidney profited well for having aligned himself with me, as I had profited earlier from the mentorship of others.

Then, some years later, when raising super cows in Central California, I took the young Daniel Pritzker under my wing. Within a year, just as I had promised his parents, I returned Daniel to his family a more focused and disciplined young man, ready to assume a respectable position in the family hierarchy. By now, you have read about Zoli Aharoni, who credits me with mentoring him and teaching him how to think successfully outside of the box. Today he is one of the most dynamic entrepreneurs in my orbit, and I continue to partner with him on a number of innovative projects.

Having significantly benefited all my life from mentorship — as both mentor and mentee — I have a keen respect for the practice. My most recent forays into the process concern an extraordinary brother and sister, whose lives were changed dramatically when our paths first crossed about a dozen years ago.

Polina, Then and Now

One day in 2004, Polina Chebotareva walked into my office and asked me for a job. I had never seen her before, nor had she bothered to make an appointment. She admitted that she had zero experience in the business world, outside of her sales job at Neiman-Marcus. But she was prepared to do any sort of office work to prove herself. No chore was too menial. The essential thing was to learn the business — if necessary, from the rock bottom, although she had no intention of staying down there for long. Her grooming, poise, and body language spoke volumes about her self-confidence. She wore her highlighted blonde hair casually to the shoulders, her makeup barely visible, yet highly professional — and her sleeveless sheath dress was a study in understated elegance. Born in 1984, Polina was no more than twenty at the time and yet she exuded the sophistication and instincts of someone decades older.

By the time she was finished allowing me to interview her, I was left with no valid reason to turn her down. During the first few weeks of her apprenticeship, Polina was forever doing the right thing — digesting information and fine-tuning her reactions. Not only was she smart and a fast learner, she was also likeable, loyal, hard-working, ambitious, and reliable. What could I do but mentor her and be grateful for the opportunity?

Born and raised in Russia, Polina had arrived in the United States with her family when she was ten. They settled in Mission Viejo in Orange County, where Polina and her two brothers attended school. Eventually, having graduated from the University of California at Irvine with a major in economics, Polina was ready to make her mark upon the business world.

Despite the fifty-three years difference in our ages — I am old enough to be her grandfather — we found we were highly compatible. Over the course of thirteen years, Polina absorbed everything I could teach her about real estate investing and development, which is considerable. I found her especially gifted at finding potential investors and then convincing them it was in their best interests to invest with our company.

Besides Polina's native intelligence and her determination to succeed, one of her greatest gifts is the flawless image she presents to the world. Still in her early twenties when she started making enough money to afford a high-end automobile, she went out and bought one of the finest sedans on the market. Often she would be approached by curious strangers asking how such a young woman was able to manage the car's costly upkeep. She would merely tell them the truth, about how she had begun in real estate with one of my companies, Berkley Enterprises, Inc., and how they could profit similarly. A number of those who took her advice became her staunchest investors. And because of Polina's power of persuasion, her luxury sedan turned into one of her wisest investments, and paid for itself many times over.

Polina's CV on the company website justly described her as "an innovative pioneer with a comprehensive background in business, economics, architecture and investments. In September 2006, she established Posh Development LLC and completed over a dozen custom homes in California and Nevada." By late 2007, she was leading numerous land development projects, and by June 2009, she was elected Vice President of Cambridge Companies — one of our offshoot organizations.

The busier she is, the more time Polina finds to pursue her passions in charitable causes, art, and culture. She is an underwriter and major donor at Harvesters Food Bank in Orange County, a board member at the Laguna Art Museum in Laguna Beach, and has helped raise awareness and funding for environmental issues. In addition, she devotes time and resources to the Village of Hope Rescue Mission, which helps bring stability to the lives of struggling families. Along the way, Polina met the love of her life, and married him in 2016.

Filipp, the Genius Brother

All the while Polina was becoming a successful businesswoman, her brilliant brother, Filipp Chebotareva, was working a nine-to-five existence and growing increasingly curious about how his sister, smart as she was, had elevated her financial holdings so far above his own. And in such record time. Eventually, I agreed to meet with him, as much out of curiosity as a willingness to help. Not surprisingly, our initial get-together went as well as mine had with his sister, a few years earlier. But would I be as lucky with my latest mentee? I looked to my instincts, as I had with Polina, and decided to take that chance. Fil not only met my expectations, he exceeded them. No less the natural businessperson than his sister, he was soon bringing in dozens of new investors to fund our company and continued to expand the brand.

Like Polina, Fil believes in community service. He sits on a number of corporate boards, including Foodstirs, Inc. and Once Upon a Farm LLC, which is a rapidly growing San

Diego-based baby food company. Fil says, "My ultimate motivators are the relationships in my life: my family, my friends, and the ability to give back to my community. I do what I say … and I keep integrity at the core of everything I do."

࿐࿐࿐

As many successful young entrepreneurs tend to do after a while, Polina and Fil began seeking out challenging new frontiers to conquer — which indicates I did a pretty good job of setting them on their ways. Of course, were it not for their innate abilities, their integrity, and their dedication and hard work, our association could never have created such a phenomenal result.

Mentorship may provide the match and light the fire, but responsibility for keeping the flame alive is completely in the hands of the individual.

࿐࿐࿐

Summing Up

It takes only one simple action on any given day to shift the course of your existence. Because Polina took that proactive first step into my office that day, she changed her life and that of her brother, as well as everyone in their immediate circle, including me.

Fil and Polina are now partnering on their own, raising $100 million in funding for, among other things, a new organic health food snack containing fresh fruits and nuts.

Tosi, as it is called, is currently being sold at point-of-purchase locations in supermarkets throughout the country. Both nutritious and delicious, it all but sells itself. Of course, with Polina and Fil on board to spread the word, it will soon be on the tip of everyone's tongue — precisely where it does its best work.

Is it any wonder that mentorship is one of the oldest and strongest relationships? And, despite recent innovations in the field of communications, there is still no connection more powerful than face-to-face contact — in person.

ॐॐॐ

The greatest good you can do for another is not to just share your riches, but to reveal to him his own.

~ Benjamin Disraeli

ॐॐॐ

CHAPTER 24

THE DOUBLY REWARDING ACT OF PRE-ZONING

Every child is a gifted child...

~ Toru Kumon

৵৵৵

What exactly is "pre-zoning"? Don't look for the word in the dictionary because I concocted the concept shortly before writing this chapter — although if it were to appear in *Webster's* someday, it might read something like this:

Pre-zone: verb. 1) to seek out the specialness in a young person and nurture it to its full potential; 2) to minimize, delay, or nullify the need to rezone

I see pre-zoning as a precursor to rezoning or, ideally, a substitute, geared toward modifying the process or replacing it entirely. In reading the preceding chapters, you may have found it obvious that rezoning is an excellent tool for improving on something that already exists. But in many cases, it is possible to avoid that life-altering step simply through early observation and training. I believe there is no greater hint at a person's potential than those signs that show up in childhood. And if you do it right with your children in those crucial first months and years of their lives, you have helped them set their career goals in stone by the time they reach maturity. In that way, they may never have a need to rezone, except within their original field of choice. Sure, they can modify as they go, as new options evolve that necessitate or favor change. But once they have found their passion and mastered it well enough to satisfy themselves and even some segment of society, they will always have a purpose and a receptive community to serve. They will always be of value.

Just as my father and grandfather were insightful enough to take notice of my talents as a child and to pre-zone me for my future life's work, each generation should be aware of their power to inspire the youngest among them — and to guide them toward polishing and perfecting their gifts.

Everyone is born with their own special talent, capable of making the world a better place. If all the untapped creativity in the world were harnessed to the maximum, the effect it would have on our planet would be incalculable. And it doesn't require genius. We can do the job with everyday thinking, a trait we all have in common. Unfortunately, some of us underestimate our capabilities, or we don't stop to envision the possibilities. We might even choose to ignore them.

While Mihaly Csikszentmihalyi was studying a group of geniuses for his book, *Creativity*, he came upon a statistic that changed his thinking about these creative giants. Whereas he found no one with an IQ below 130 to have changed the world, that lofty potential was uniformly accessible for anyone within the range of 130 to 170. As Malcolm Gladwell suggested in *Outliers*, "good enough" is capable of yielding the same results as "extraordinary." We also know that the harder you work, the more likely you are to achieve your goals.

Signs of Potential Greatness

If you think your child has special talents or shows obvious signs of precociousness — over and above the usual "cuteness" quotient — help substantiate your suspicions with the following partial checklist of positive traits. Does (or is) he or she:

- uncommonly alert, even as an infant
- a quick learner
- verbally communicative
- self-taught in reading and writing skills
- a problem solver
- an abstract thinker
- highly sensitive
- ask probing questions
- have a sharp memory
- have a keen sense of humor
- have a vivid imagination
- think outside of the box
- possess an early set of ethics
- have an advanced attention span
- tend to be a daydreamer
- have an uncommon curiosity

This list was compiled from a number of professional sources, along with a good dose of personal observation and common sense. Don't be disappointed if your child doesn't conform to every one of these characteristics. Even the presence of a precious few of these traits may be all you need to confirm your expectations.

It Runs in the Family

It is true that some gifts are easier to spot than others. My own were no mystery to anyone, including myself. I made it patently clear as a child that I loved things electronic and scientific. But if my grandfather had not taken the time to bring out that aspect of me, I might not have chosen as wisely as I grew into adulthood. Conscious choices aside, electronics took me just so far in life. Fortunately, my father, who had already tapped into my keen interest in real estate development, helped bridge the gap for me. After that, with the support of a mentor or two, my willingness to work two jobs simultaneously, and my determination to succeed, I was soon confidently on my own and capable of inspiring others. What had been there from the start, however, were my imagination and curiosity — the essential traits of an entrepreneur, ready to adapt to new opportunities and willing to take on the inherent risks.

When my kids were small, I would often take them to one or another of my construction sites. That early influence stayed with them, and when they grew up, two of my sons chose to follow in my footsteps. They have both been successful over the years, and, from what I am told, they never regretted their decision. As I mentioned earlier, my eldest son was the exception. His natural passion for music was the path he took from the start, and from which he has never wavered. My daughter's life choice to create a family of her own was perhaps inspired by the loving domestic atmosphere in which she grew up. So, all four of my children are at a place in life where they want to be. And that is the ultimate goal.

As a teenager, my grandson showed promise as a fashion designer. Because he lives in Los Angeles and makes friends easily, he meets famous women from time to time who commission him to design their wardrobe for one grand occasion or another. I encouraged him from the beginning, underwrote his first collection, and continue to help him whenever he needs me. This is Jonathan's gift — his chosen life's work. Fortunately he has received well-deserved praise for his talents. Praise is like that. It fosters the confidence to pursue your dreams.

Even as the father of four, I am not an expert on child development. But I do know that parents, grandparents, and teachers can have a powerful influence on the younger generation. That is why I feel it is incumbent upon them to watch closely for their children's proclivities and provide them with the proper environment in which to grow.

Without early encouragement, Wolfgang Amadeus Mozart would not likely have taught himself the harpsichord when he was three or composed his first piece of music at five or six. Although he died prematurely at age thirty-five, he left an enormous legacy of six hundred compositions, which the world continues to enjoy. Before Pablo Picasso could speak, the story goes, he showed an inclination toward his artist father's profession — and by the time he could express himself in words, he demanded the use of his elder's paintbrushes. Father of the cubist school, Picasso is now considered the greatest painter of the twentieth century. These are but two of the many gifted individuals, famous and otherwise, who, within a wide variety of fields, achieved greatness in their lifetimes. But genius and accomplishment are two separate qualities, and one does not automatically follow the other.

Perhaps some geniuses have been too smart for their own good and their parental pressure far too intense, ultimately giving way to negative outcomes. One example is Theodore Kaczynski (aka the Unabomber), who was enrolled at Harvard University at age sixteen with an impressive IQ of 167. By the time he was twenty-five, he had earned his doctorate degree and became the youngest teacher at the University of California at Berkeley. Two years later, he resigned from his post. The rest of his story reads like a movie script. Kaczynski left the home of his parents, moved into the woods, and pursued a twenty-year career in mail bombing before the authorities caught up with him. By then he was responsible for the death of three people and injury to twenty-three more. Another prodigy gone wrong due to overbearing — and, in the case of the father, unprincipled — parents is Sufiah Yusof, who, at sixteen, was admitted to Oxford University for her genius in math. Apparently she and her parents had conflicting visions of her future, and she ran away from school in protest. Following a short-lived marriage, she began a career in prostitution. Currently, she is employed as a social worker, having never lived up to her exceptional potential. So, as I already suggested, geniuses do not always deliver the goods, especially when their choices are controlled by outside forces. And sometimes, especially when passion and purpose are present, the efforts of more "average" people tend to outshine them.

Major things sometimes happen to people, despite their minor expectations. Pierre Omidyar began a website, precursor to eBay, in his San Jose living room over a Labor Day weekend in 1995. He had no ambitions of becoming an internet tycoon. His online site was intended as nothing more than a device to assist people in selling their goods and services. Three years later when he and his business partner, Jeff Skoll, brought in branding expert Meg Whitman, the company took on its current name, eBay, expanded exponentially, and eventually made Omidyar a multi-billionaire.

Craig Newmark, self-professed nerd, began prophesizing about the internet to his friends and associates as early as the 1980s. One day in 1995, he sent out an email to ten friends with news from his native San Francisco. That email soon blossomed into an information exchange that grew and kept growing until it turned into craigslist.com, one of the earlier successes on the internet, and still highly active. Thus far, craigslist, even without ads, has made its founder $380 million. Like Omidyar, Newmark possessed a background in technology, but hadn't a clue that by applying his knowledge and expertise he would create a phenomenal business model.

To illustrate that brilliance does not always result in miracles, take the case of the Almighty God on Mount Sinai in his legendary conversation with Moses. After giving the Jewish leader the eternal principles of the Ten Commandments, God told Moses to take them back to his people that they might use them as a guidepost for living. But He knew Moses had a speech impediment, which would have made it difficult for him to express himself effectively. Did He take this important occasion to cure Moses of his inability to communicate properly, which, being God, should have been a simple enough task to perform? No. Instead he told Moses to give the commandments to his brother, Aaron, who, in turn, would deliver His message. So, ultimately, one has to wonder about the limitations of anyone — even God.

The Gift of Giving

But there is another gift of perhaps even greater value, and it has little to do with career and everything to do with the quality of your character. And that is the gift of humanity — kindness, charity, compassion, benevolence, love, gratitude, and forgiveness. This gift is not linked to your intellect, or education, or hard work. It is merely an extension of your nature, and yet it is bound to reward you with greater happiness, fulfillment, and lasting relationships than genius alone ever could do. And, as I've already stated previously, you have only to share it generously every day for the rest of your life.

෯෯෯

Set a goal so big that you can't achieve it until you grow into the person who can.

~ Unknown

ॐॐॐ

At times, talented is gifted! But mostly it comes with good practice.

~ Somya Kedia

ॐॐॐ

FINAL THOUGHTS

Imagination is more important than knowledge. For knowledge is limited, whereas imagination embraces the entire world, stimulating progress, giving birth to revolution.

~ Albert Einstein

☙☙☙

As a rezone-in-training, it is your task to look at everything around you from a new perspective. People, places, and things may appear on first glance to be the obvious, but the more you view them through the lens of your vivid imagination, the greater the possibilities emerge. This is what separates you from the rest of the population and places you in the company of geniuses, innovators, achievers, and merely extraordinary doers and thinkers — just like yourself.

What do you see when you drive along the ocean? Do you stare straight ahead at the road, without a fleeting glance at the sun setting behind the horizon or the exquisite gardens in the foreground? If so, think how much you are missing out on life's experiences.

The world around you is what you call upon to solve a problem or inspire a new idea or expand upon an old one. The more closely you remain in contact with its wonders, the more abundant the flow of your creative juices. For example, nothing feeds my imagination more than taking the dog for a walk in the neighborhood or driving down a country road. But you don't even have to leave home for a brisk mental outing. Simply seat yourself in a relaxing position, play some inspiring music, breathe to the tempo, and turn on your brain. You will be amazed by the images, ideas, and innovations that move on through that higher center of learning of yours every second of the day and night. All that is required of you is that you pay close attention.

One recommendation for generating a never-ending source of ideas is to follow the cardinal rule of James Altucher, entrepreneur and bestselling author of *The Power of No* and *Choose Yourself.* He makes a list of ten different ideas every day of the week — every week of the year — every year of his life. And he strongly advocates for this strategy, as it has worked so well for him in the past. These ideas of yours can be completely random notions that, on the surface, at least, lack cohesion. And that's okay. What you are doing is greasing the wheels. Over time, at least one of those concepts will present you with a creative breakthrough, brimming with dazzling prospects. I would also suggest brainstorming ideas with others. Sometimes, one person has the flash of an idea, but it takes someone else to light the fuse. And often you have no conscious awareness of the process. You can be buying a gallon of milk at the corner market or watching a tennis match, or attending a birthday party, or watching an old movie, or picking the kids up from school. Something suddenly strikes a chord, and your mind grabs onto it with gusto. Will you explore it, or will you discard it for being impractical? We have no concept of how many viable ideas we have on a daily basis, nor the capacity they have to change our lives — or the lives of others. Become more vigilant and immerse yourself in the potential that surrounds you.

Children, too, need a regimen to optimize their creative thinking. You can help them formulate theirs by exposing them to such phenomena as nature, science, books, art, music, and people. Eventually they will find the path to those things for which they have the greatest affinity. Once you have your clues, do what you can to further inspire them on the subject, and encourage them to incorporate whatever it is into their lives. Feeling special can be a lifelong blessing, and you have the power to spark that in your children, giving them the confidence to meet the challenges they face in the future.

Sometimes imagination and preparedness get together with pure luck — as what happened to me more than half a century ago with the city council member and the London Fog raincoat. And then you are off and sprinting toward your inevitable success. True, sometimes limitation stands in the way of luck, and that's when you have to double up on the imagination and preparedness — which is, to a great extent, what luck is all about.

I hope that sharing my experiences and insights will inspire you to a fresh perspective on this planet, as you discover new concepts you had overlooked, new ways to perceive them, and innovative ways to develop them.

৵৵৵

Everyone must leave something behind when he dies ... Something your hand touched some way so your soul has somewhere to go when you die ... It doesn't matter what you do, so long as you change something from the way it was before you touched it into something that's like you after you take your hands away.

~ Ray Bradbury, Fahrenheit 451

❧ ❧ ❧

ODES TO A FEW EXTRAORDINARY PEOPLE

࿐࿐࿐

Following are three odes I have written over the years — from nonsensical to sublime — for extraordinary people who, in one way or another, had a transformative effect on my life. Please humor me by reading them through. They might generate a smile or inspire a sigh.

1. To demonstrate my respect and admiration for Zoli Aharoni, I wrote him the following zany verse in classic iambic pentameter:

ZOLI AHARONI: ODE TO A DAREDEVIL DUDE

࿐࿐࿐

Zoli Aharoni when he was young
Couldn't speak the English tongue
In Tel Aviv where he was born
He spoke just Hebrew night and morn.
Zoli Aharoni grew up forlorn
Filled with anger and with scorn.
Because he was born with *one* hand — not two.
Now, *you* tell *me*. Wouldn't that make *you* blue?
But, Zoli Aharoni had a brilliant mind
And a heart of gold — the giving kind
He wouldn't let his missing hand

Hold him back from being grand.
So, with Zoli Aharoni's lofty intentions
He set out to create exciting inventions.
At work in Las Vegas he's always busy
Innovating so much it would make you dizzy.
One day Zoli bought a piece of real estate
The price was so cheap — it was hard to contemplate
Then he sold it for a million bucks
Talk about beginner's luck.
Zoli did something else profound
When he buried a powerline underground
To make it possible to build a store
And bank a cool three million more.
Zoli Aharoni — his latest facet
Transforming bathrooms from liability to asset
A bathroom was once where you *needed* to go
Now it's where you *want* to go.
Zoli is wise — like the Dalai Lama
Which is how he invented his Naturama
The magic liquid that melts fat and oil —
It's so easy to do, you don't have to toil.
His latest idea is extra bright
The shoes he designed with a special light
For children to wear all night and day
And connect with their parents while they're at play.
Zoli Aharoni's a slogan writer
His latest one could not be tighter
"Live green — Heaven can wait."™

The green industry has sealed his fate.
Zoli Aharoni is a man of vision
Always making the right decision.
Esteemed and loved by everyone around him,
Especially those women who forever surround him.

ॐॐॐ

2. In honor of Victor, my Australian real estate colleague in
    Las Vegas, I wrote the following nonsensical poem — even
    wackier than the ode I wrote to Zoli. In good times and bad,
    we all need to laugh, even at the silliest things. No doubt,
    Bob Stupak would have agreed. I suspect you will, as well.

VISIONARY VICTOR'S VANISHING VICTORY

A Versified Vignette

ॐॐॐ

A Vainglorious Visitor named Victor Vas Vocal about his Vivid
Vision
That Vertical Valuable condos Vith Views and Vistas
Vould be Very Voguish in Vegas.
Verily, Victor Vas the Valid Vanguard of Vertical Villas
And Ventured Vigorously Vithin the Visible
Venue of the Vegas Valley Vicinity
Vith Vast Velocity and Voracity.

Vexingly, he Vanted to Vin Vith a Vengeance
But his Vigor Vas all in Vain.

Once he began Vacillating he Vas Virtually Vanquished.
His Vapid Ventures Vere Vaporizing and Void
Like Varicose Veins, Vasectomies, and Vulgar Vintage Vaccinations.
True, he Vas Vulnerable — in a Virtual Vacuum Vortex — but
not yet Vanished Vrom the Vacuous Venue.

Vun day a Voice Vispered to the Venerable Victor
To use his Vast Vitality, Verve, and Vunderous Voodoo
To abandon his Voluminous Vagaries — his Veritable Vanities
And Varied Vices — like his Valuable Varnished Vehicles
Or his Versace Valises and Variegated Velvet Vestments by
Valentino —
To Veto his Vagrancy and Valiantly Value his Versatility.
That's the Vun Verifiable Vay to Viable Victory
In life's Varied Vicissitudes.

Vithout Venting, Victor, I Vow Vulgarity and Vitriol has
Videly Vacated my Vocabulary;
I don't Vilify or Vindicate or, Verst of all, Vituperate Venom-
ously in the Vernacular.
But Victor, it is time to say, Vociferously, "Vuck it"!
I am Virile, Vigorous, and Vigilant
And — not to Vaticinate here — but I Vouchsafe to Vamp up,
not to Veer, from my own Vascinating Voyage — nor, God
Vorbid — to Vegetate into Victimhood.
I Vill build Vibrating, Versatile, Viable, Voluminous Vital Ver-
tical Villas Vested in Vegas.

And that's ... Vor sure! *Vavoom!*

Vith Vehemently Varm Vishes and Viva Las Vegas Virtues ...
Verever you are.
Vrom your Vriend, Michael Bash,
Victor's Verbose and Vocal Versifier — Vorevermore

ॐॐॐ

3. Because of the difference Polina has made in the way I con-
    duct my business — she breathed new life into it before
    and after the crash of 2008 — I chose my favorite way of
    honoring her. I wrote her a poem. This one:

Polina

May 2, 2009

ॐॐॐ

God made a wonderful woman,
A woman who'll never grow old.
He fashioned her smile like sunshine
And molded her heart of pure gold.
He formed her eyes like shimmering stars,
And set her bright spirit free.
God made a wonderful woman,
And he sent this woman to me.

I will always be most grateful to God
For Polina, His precious gift.

Her goal is to make me happy
And to cause my spirit to lift.

A smart and stylish young lady,
The quintessence of elegance and chic,
She can also cook up a gourmet meal
That is truthfully magnifique!
Her virtues, her charms are legion.
Her aura fills me with glee.
God made this beautiful woman
And he sent her, with blessings, to me.

~ Michael

ACKNOWLEDGMENTS

꩜꩜꩜

I thank the many people, who, over the course of my eighty-seven years, mentored, inspired, and supported me — making it possible to live out my dreams and document my collective insights and experiences.

My grandfather taught me religious principles and helped cultivate my moral center as well as my curiosity for the sciences. Mother was my greatest supporter, always fighting for my best interests as I grew into maturity. Father consistently approved of my key decisions, including my choice to migrate to the United States for a superior education in engineering. He later supported my decision to rezone as a real estate developer, mentoring me and providing me with my initial investors.

My beloved wife, Arlene, gave me the love and solid home life on which I thrived, along with four healthy and happy children — all of whom, as adults, have played an active role in my life: Joel, Jeremy, David, and Sharon.

My dear late brother, Yigal, was a trusted sibling in childhood and a valuable partner on a number of projects as an adult.

I also thank my grandson, Jonathan, for his companionship and inspiration, and younger grandson, Joshua, in whom I hold lofty hopes for the future.

Finally, I am thankful to the rest of my colleagues and acquaintances who have played a pivotal role in my life, many of whom are depicted in these chapters. Without them, this book might never have been written. A partial list includes: Charlie Patrick, Rupert Murdoch, Danny Thomas, the Pritzker family, Tony Robbins, Zoli Aharoni, Polina Cherabotev, Filipp Cherabotev, and my treasured secretary, Janice McCown, who has been of enormous help throughout this process.

Thanks, as well, to Roberta Edgar, who has a fine flair for translating my thoughts, ideas, and experiences into the printed word.

~ Michael Bash

ॐॐॐ

My thanks go to those collaborators, mentors, friends, family members, and associates who, by trusting in my talent over the years, helped me to elevate the quality of my writing. Among them are: Mary Thompson, Nicky Noxon, June Burakoff Smith, Cheryl Edgar Ryan, Renée Tener Hertzberg, Manny Diez, Duke Libby, Paolo Ficara, Flo Selfman (partner at wordsalamode.com), Jean-Noel Bassior (speakerservices.com), and my fellow members of Independent Writers of Southern California (iwosc.org), who inspired me to rezone from screenwriting to developing and writing books. Most of all, I thank Michael Bash, whose faith in my ability to tell his story precisely as he would have it told ultimately vaulted me over the finish line.

~ Roberta Edgar

ॐॐॐ

ABOUT THE AUTHOR:
MICHAEL BASH

꙰꙰꙰

Michael E. Bash, founder of Cambridge Companies, headquartered in Las Vegas, Nevada, started his career in the real estate and land development arena over fifty-five years ago. As a young engineer Bash had an understanding of how things worked and fit together, although he had already discovered his talents as a young boy in his native pre-Israel Jerusalem.

After borrowing $30,000 from a friend of his father to finance his first real estate deal, Bash was immediately hooked on the industry. He profited so well from the loan that a few years later, prior to his thirty-second birthday, he officially became a millionaire. Since then, he has been involved with major planning and zoning projects and building and developing a number of shopping centers, hundreds of homes, office buildings, water and sewer systems, and nearly 6,000 apartment units and condos throughout New York State. He also participated in building the Laniado Hospital in Netanya, Israel, and is one of the founders and contributors to the Jerusalem Great Synagogue.

Actively involved in charity work and politics, Mr. Bash served as financial advisor to then President Jimmy Carter as part of the Democratic National Finance Committee and later as advisor to President George H. W. Bush. He financed several telethons for St. Jude Children's Hospital, which continues to raise several million dollars annually to cover critical medical procedures for children, and he is occasionally interviewed on various cable networks, such as CNN and Fox.

Bash's second passion is writing. His book topics include investment, history, science, and the Bible. The most recently published is *Evolution by God*, which discusses a path toward achieving harmony between science and religion. Visit the website at www.evolutionbygod.com for additional information or to order a copy.

కింకింకిం

About the Co-Author: Roberta Edgar

Roberta Edgar is a writer, editor, story analyst, consultant, and ghostwriter, as well as a (reformed) screenwriter. After UCLA graduation, Roberta was hired by literary/fashion magazine *Mademoiselle* to help plan themes for monthly issues and to coordinate annual fashion shows at the Plaza Hotel. In addition to working on network TV series, including *Star Trek* (the original) and *The FBI*, she wrote episodes for Norman Lear's short-lived series, *All That Glitters*. Roberta also has a number of unproduced screenplays to her discredit as well as a stack of unfinished books. (Such is the life of a busy ghostwriter.) She is also actively involved with Independent Writers of Southern California. Visit Roberta at www.wordsalamode.com.

కింకింకిం

www.ingramcontent.com/pod-product-compliance
Lightning Source LLC
LaVergne TN
LVHW051451080426
835509LV00017B/1737